Economic Political and Financial Analyses

By:
Musabekov Sherali

© Taemeer Publications LLC
Economic Political and Financial Analyses
by: Musabekov Sherali
Edition: August '2023
Publisher:
Taemeer Publications LLC (Michigan, USA / Hyderabad, India)

ISBN 978-93-5872-137-9

© Taemeer Publications

Book	:	*Economic Political and Financial Analyses*
Author	:	**Musabekov Sherali**
Publisher	:	Taemeer Publications
Year	:	'2023
Pages	:	112
Title Design	:	*Taemeer Web Design*

Table of Content

CHAPTER I.

1. Analysis of Current Trends and the Role of Small and Large Businesses in International Market Competition.
2. Existing issues with small business expansion: solutions and directions for improvement.
3. The economic costs of the Russia-Ukraine conflict.

CHAPTER II.

1. Economic implications of the Russia-Ukraine conflict on EU economic policy, including fiscal support and monetary monitoring.

CHAPTER III.

1. The main problems faced by business entities operating in the territory of Uzbekistan.
2. The economic effect of monetary policy for the economy and its role in the economy.
3. Reasons and consequences of joining the World Trade Organization and the Republic of Uzbekistan.
4. The Role of Digital Finance and Technological Innovation in the Growth of the Green Economy

REVIEW

Ensuring the development of the economy in the selected Uzbekistan fully corresponds to the concept of the state system and the priorities of the modern economy based on international standards. Based on this, it can be said that the chosen topic is relevant.

Written on the topic of the development of the economy in Uzbekistan, this book consists of an introduction, a main chapter and a conclusion, and is covered in the form of economic accounts and specific facts:

Topic 1: Analysis of current trends and large enterprises in small and international market competition;

Topic 2: Existing problems with small business expansion: solutions and improvement areas

Topic 3: Economic costs of the Russian-Ukrainian conflict.

Topic 4: Economic impacts of the Russian-Ukrainian conflict on the economic policy of the European Union with fiscal support and monetary monitoring

Topic 5: The main problems faced by economic entities in Uzbekistan are the main ones

Topic 6: The economic effect of the monetary economy on the economy and its role in the economy.

Topic 7: Causes and consequences of joining the World Trade Organization and the Republic of Uzbekistan

Topic 8: The Role of Digital Finance and Technological Innovation in the Growth of the Green Economy

On this topic, sufficient data on the analysis of the development of the economy in Uzbekistan is indicated and revealed on the basis of calculations. I note that there are no gross shortcomings in the introductory part, the main part and conclusions presented above. In this regard, the book on the topic "The development of the economy in Uzbekistan" was prepared at the required level.

Introduction

The 2030 Agenda for Sustainable Development (2030 Agenda) presents an ambitious, complex and interconnected vision that countries around the world have committed to working towards. Countries face several challenges in developing an integrated approach to financing the SDGs. Mobilizing the scale of public and private resources required while maximizing their impact on social, environmental and economic dimensions of the 2030 Agenda presents a range of challenges, from managing complex financing instruments, to designing and implementing effective policies, and collaborating with a diverse range of actors. These challenges are often rooted in, or made more difficult by, misalignment between the planning and finance policy functions of government, as well as the participation of only a narrow group of stakeholders in dialogue and decisions on financing. United Nations' Member states recognized these challenges of SDG financing in the Addis Ababa Action Agenda. The 2019 Financing for Sustainable Development Report recommends countries to consider developing Integrated National Financing Frameworks (INFFs) to support their national development strategies. INFFs support shifting financing perspective towards long-term investment horizons and integrating sustainability as a central concern of investment decisions. It enables aligning private and public incentives with sustainable development, and better measuring the impacts on sustainability. The 2019 Financing for Sustainable Development Report recommends countries to consider developing Integrated National Financing Frameworks (INFFs) to support their national development strategies. INFFs support shifting financing perspective towards long-term investment horizons and integrating sustainability as a central concern of investment decisions. It enables aligning private and public incentives with sustainable development, and better measuring the impacts on sustainability. The 2019 Financing for Sustainable Development Report recommends countries to consider developing Integrated National Financing Frameworks (INFFs) to support their national development strategies. INFFs support shifting financing perspective towards long-term investment horizons and integrating sustainability as a central concern of investment decisions.

In the conditions of rapidly developing reality, each state determines its firm stance and effective ways of development. In this context, the independent Uzbekistan needed to objectively assess the historical development path of the young independent state, the accumulated experience and analyze the progress made, identify measures to further enhance democratic reforms, set priorities for accelerated development of the country and clear goals. The mentioned objectives were preceded by practical talks, discussions with the broad public, representatives of the business community, leaders and experts of state bodies. They reviewed legislative acts, information and analytical resources of local and international organizations, recommendations and comments, as well as studied the experience of developed foreign countries. The proposals, their study and generalization built the basis for the National Action Strategy for Five Priority Development Areas in 2017-2021 and other programs that have mapped out the fate of the state for the near future. The Action Strategy is divided into five stages, each of which will be carried out as a separate annual State program. The first stage of reforms was reflected in the State Program on the Implementation of the National Action Strategy for Five Priority Development Areas in 2017-2021 in the Year of

Dialogue with the People and Human Interests. In this regard, the reforms in the framework of the Action Strategy accentuated the implementation of the tasks identified in the State Program. The effective implementation of 437 actions, consisting of 320 articles, adoption of 29 laws and more than 900 other legislative acts have resulted in certain positive changes in all areas of life of the state and society. In 2017, many initiatives of the head of state on the reborn of state authority and administration, judicial and legal system, agriculture, oil and gas, chemical, mining, energy, construction, architectural industries, road and transport communications, pharmaceuticals, textiles, tourism, information technologies, as well as integrated socio-economic development of the regions have been practically supported by people. The guarantees for protecting citizens' rights and freedoms have been strengthened. The measures within the framework of state and regional programs were aimed at solving the problems of people's concern that relate to everyday life. The objectives of ensuring the balance between the state and society, adoption of new technologies of public administration, improvement of public administration, and creation of decent living conditions for people are being effectively fulfilled. The consistent follow-up of the liberalization and reform processes in all areas of society remains a priority. Pressing problems in all areas and branches have been openly discussed with the population, and addressed. The adoption of all decisions based on the opinions and appeals of the people proved key in prompt and effective implementation of reforms. The streamlined procedure of providing information and reports in the economic, banking and financial institutions, in utilities sector, internal and foreign affairs, education and upbringing, public health, parliamentary and local councils, judicial and legal system allowed introducing public control in practice. Initiated by the President, fundamental reforms and actions in all areas of state and society life have further strengthened the entrepreneurial trends in people, strengthened their civil position, expanded the involvement of each person in state and public management. Official decisions are getting more focused on human interests. This edition consists of five main sections, each of which covers each of the five priority areas of the Action Strategy. It draws your attention aiming to highlight the ongoing reforms in the country in 2017, and to convey their idea and importance to the general public. It thoroughly and profoundly analyzes the reforms that have been implemented at the initiative of the President of the Republic of Uzbekistan Shavkat Mirziyoyev throughout 2017 in all areas of life of the state and society. The information is represented as short observations and infographics. This book offers information on the reforms that have been implemented in all areas of life in the country over the past year, and is seen as important to the general public.

CHAPTER I. Analysis of Current Trends and the Role of Small and Large Businesses in International Market Competition.

Small and large businesses play a significant role in international market competition. They contribute to economic growth, job creation, innovation, and trade. However, the dynamics between small and large businesses in the global market are complex, with both opportunities and challenges. This article aims to analyze the role of small and large businesses in international market competition and explore current trends that impact their competitiveness.

Role of Small Businesses in International Market Competition: Small businesses have traditionally faced challenges when competing with large multinational corporations in the global market. However, they also bring unique advantages that contribute to their competitiveness: Niche Markets Small businesses often specialize in niche markets, catering to specific customer segments or offering specialized products or services. This allows them to differentiate themselves from larger competitors and target customers with specific needs or preferences.

Agility and Adaptability: Small businesses are typically more agile and adaptable compared to large corporations. They can quickly respond to changes in market conditions, consumer trends, or regulatory requirements. This flexibility enables small businesses to seize emerging opportunities and adjust their strategies accordingly. Innovation and Creativity: Small businesses are often at the forefront of innovation and creativity. They have the ability to experiment with new ideas, develop unique solutions, and disrupt established markets. This innovative spirit allows small businesses to challenge the status quo and create competitive advantages.

Local Market Knowledge: Small businesses often have a deep understanding of local markets, including cultural nuances, consumer preferences, and regulatory environments. This knowledge gives them an edge when competing against larger corporations that may struggle to navigate unfamiliar markets.

Despite these advantages, small businesses face several challenges in international market competition: Limited Resources: Small businesses often have limited financial resources, making it difficult to invest in research and development, marketing campaigns, or international expansion. Limited resources can also hinder their ability to compete on price or scale. Access to Distribution Channels: Small businesses may face challenges in accessing international distribution channels, particularly in highly regulated industries or markets dominated by large distributors. Limited access to distribution networks can restrict their reach and affect their competitiveness.

Brand Recognition: Building brand recognition and establishing a strong reputation in international markets can be challenging for small businesses. Larger corporations often have established brands and extensive marketing budgets, making it difficult for small businesses to compete on brand awareness. Lack of Economies of Scale: Small businesses may struggle to achieve economies of scale, which can result in higher production costs compared to larger competitors. This cost disadvantage can affect their ability to compete on price and profitability. Role of Large Businesses in International Market Competition: Large businesses, particularly multinational corporations, play a dominant role in international market competition. They have significant advantages that contribute to their competitiveness: Global Reach: Large businesses have extensive global networks, distribution channels, and supply chains, allowing them to reach customers in multiple countries. This global reach provides them with economies of scale and the ability to leverage their size and resources. Financial Resources: Large businesses typically have access to substantial financial resources, enabling them to invest in research and development, marketing campaigns, acquisitions, and international expansion. This financial strength gives them a competitive edge over smaller businesses. Large businesses typically have access to substantial financial resources, enabling them to invest in research and development, marketing campaigns, acquisitions, and international expansion. This financial strength gives them a competitive edge over smaller businesses. Large businesses typically have access to substantial financial resources, enabling them to invest in research and development, marketing campaigns, acquisitions, and international expansion.

This financial strength gives them a competitive edge over smaller businesses.

Established Brands: Large businesses often have well-known brands with strong brand recognition and customer loyalty. Established brands provide a competitive advantage by influencing consumer perceptions, trust, and purchasing decisions.

Operational Efficiency: Large businesses can achieve operational efficiency through standardized processes, automation, and economies of scale. This efficiency allows them to produce goods or deliver services at lower costs compared to smaller competitors.

Despite these advantages, large businesses also face challenges in international market competition. Bureaucracy and Decision-Making Processes: Large businesses often face challenges associated with bureaucracy and slow decision- making processes. These challenges can hinder their ability to respond quickly to market changes or adapt to local market needs.

Lack of Flexibility: Large businesses may struggle to be as agile and flexible as smaller competitors. Their size and complex organizational structures can make it difficult to implement changes or respond to emerging trends in a timely manner.

Risk Aversion: Large businesses may be more risk-averse compared to small businesses. This risk aversion can limit their willingness to experiment with new ideas, embrace disruptive technologies, or enter unfamiliar markets, potentially impacting their competitiveness.

Reputation and Public Perception: Large businesses are often under scrutiny from the public, media, and regulatory bodies. Negative publicity or public perception can damage their reputation and impact consumer trust, leading to a loss of market share or competitive disadvantage. Current Trends Impacting Small and Large Businesses in International Market Competition Several current trends are shaping the dynamics between small and large businesses in international market competition. Digital Transformation: The rapid advancement of digital technologies is transforming business operations, customer interactions, and market dynamics. Small businesses that embrace digital transformation can enhance their competitiveness by improving operational efficiency, reaching global markets through e-commerce,

E-commerce and Global Market Access: E-commerce platforms have democratized access to global markets, allowing small businesses to compete on a global scale. Online marketplaces enable small businesses to reach customers worldwide without the need for physical infrastructure or extensive distribution networks.

Sustainability and Corporate Social Responsibility: Consumers are increasingly demanding sustainable and socially responsible products and services. Small businesses that prioritize sustainability and corporate social responsibility can differentiate themselves from larger competitors and attract environmentally conscious consumers. Global Supply Chain Disruptions: Recent events such as the COVID-19 pandemic have highlighted the vulnerability of global supply chains. Small businesses that adopt resilient supply chain strategies, such as diversifying suppliers or embracing local sourcing, can mitigate risks and maintain a competitive advantage.

Collaborative Partnerships: Small and large businesses are increasingly forming collaborative partnerships to leverage each other's strengths and resources. Large businesses can benefit from the agility and innovation of small businesses, while small businesses can access the distribution networks and financial resources of large corporations.

Localization and Customization: The trend toward localization and customization is gaining momentum, driven by consumer preferences for personalized experiences and local products. Small businesses that can offer tailored solutions, adapt to local market needs, and provide personalized customer experiences can compete effectively against larger competitors.

Conclusion, Small and large businesses both play crucial roles in international market competition. While large businesses have advantages such as global reach, financial resources, and established brands, small businesses bring unique strengths such as niche market focus, agility, and innovation. Current trends such as digital transformation, e-commerce, sustainability, supply chain disruptions, collaborative partnerships, and localization impact the competitiveness of both small and large businesses. By understanding these dynamics and leveraging their respective strengths, small and large businesses can navigate the complexities of international market competition and thrive in a rapidly evolving global economy.

1.2 Existing issues with small business expansion: solutions and directions for improvement.

Small businesses play a crucial role in the economy, contributing to job creation, innovation, and economic growth. However, expanding a small business can be challenging due to various obstacles that hinder growth and success. These challenges can vary depending on the specific industry and circumstances, but some common problems include limited financial resources, lack of skilled workforce, ineffective marketing strategies, operational inefficiencies, scalability challenges, lack of market differentiation, and limited access to technology and innovation. In this article, we will explore potential solutions and ways of improvement for each of these challenges to help small businesses overcome barriers to expansion.

Limited financial resources: One of the most common challenges faced by small businesses when it comes to expansion is limited financial resources. Many small businesses struggle to secure funding for growth due to limited capital and difficulty accessing loans or investments. However, there are several solutions and ways of improvement that can help overcome this challenge: Explore alternative financing options: Instead of relying solely on traditional bank loans, small businesses can explore alternative financing options such as crowdfunding, angel investors, or government grants. Crowdfunding platforms provide an opportunity to raise funds from a large number of individuals who believe in the business idea or product. Angel investors, on the other hand, are individuals or groups who provide capital in exchange for equity or a stake in the business. Government grants are another option worth exploring, as they can provide financial support specifically targeted at small businesses.

Develop a detailed business plan and financial projections: To attract potential investors or lenders, small businesses should develop a detailed business plan and financial projections. A well-prepared business plan demonstrates the viability and growth potential of the business, which can increase the chances of securing funding. Financial projections should include revenue forecasts, expense estimates, and cash flow analysis to provide a clear picture of the business's financial health. Build relationships with financial institutions and investors: Small businesses can improve their chances of securing funding by building relationships with financial institutions and investors. Networking events, industry conferences, and business associations provide opportunities to connect with potential lenders or investors.

Lack of skilled workforce: Finding and retaining skilled employees can be a significant challenge for small businesses, particularly in competitive industries. However, investing in employee training and development programs, offering attractive compensation packages, flexible work arrangements, and fostering a positive work culture can help overcome this challenge. Here are some solutions and ways of improvement: Invest in employee training and development: Small businesses can invest in employee training and development programs to enhance skills and knowledge. This can include providing opportunities for employees to attend workshops, conferences, or industry-specific training programs. Offering ongoing training and development opportunities not only improves employee skills but also increases employee engagement and loyalty. Offer attractive compensation packages: Small businesses may struggle to compete with larger companies when it comes to compensation packages. However, they can offer other attractive benefits such as flexible work arrangements, work-life balance initiatives, or performance-based bonuses. By understanding the needs and preferences of employees, small businesses can tailor compensation packages that align with their values and priorities. Foster a positive work culture: A positive work culture is crucial for attracting and retaining skilled employees. Small businesses should focus on creating a supportive and inclusive work environment where employees feel valued and engaged. Encouraging open communication, recognizing and rewarding employee achievements, Small businesses may struggle to compete with larger companies when it comes to compensation packages. However, they can offer other attractive benefits such as flexible work arrangements, work-life balance initiatives, or performance-based bonuses. By understanding the needs and preferences of employees, small businesses can tailor compensation packages that align with their values and priorities. Foster a positive work culture: A positive work culture is crucial for attracting and retaining

skilled employees. Small businesses should focus on creating a supportive and inclusive work environment where employees feel valued and engaged. Encouraging open communication, recognizing and rewarding employee achievements, Small businesses may struggle to compete with larger companies when it comes to compensation packages. However, they can offer other attractive benefits such as flexible work arrangements, work-life balance initiatives, or performance-based bonuses. By understanding the needs and preferences of employees, small businesses can tailor compensation packages that align with their values and priorities. Foster a positive work culture: A positive work culture is crucial for attracting and retaining skilled employees. Small businesses should focus on creating a supportive and inclusive work environment where employees feel valued and engaged. Encouraging open communication, recognizing and rewarding employee achievements, work-life balance initiatives, or performance-based bonuses. By understanding the needs and preferences of employees, small businesses can tailor compensation packages that align with their values and priorities. Foster a positive work culture: A
positive work culture is crucial for attracting and retaining skilled employees. Small businesses should focus on creating a supportive and inclusive work environment where employees feel valued and engaged. Encouraging open communication, recognizing and rewarding employee achievements, work-life balance initiatives, or performance-based bonuses. By understanding the needs and preferences of employees, small

businesses can tailor compensation packages that align with their values and priorities. Foster a positive work culture: A positive work culture is crucial for attracting and retaining skilled employees. Small businesses should focus on creating a supportive and inclusive work environment where employees feel valued and engaged. Encouraging open communication, recognizing and rewarding employee achievements, Small businesses should focus on creating a supportive and inclusive work environment where employees feel valued and engaged. Encouraging open communication, recognizing and rewarding employee achievements, Small businesses should focus on creating a supportive and inclusive work environment where employees feel valued and engaged. Encouraging open communication, recognizing and rewarding employee achievements,

Ineffective marketing strategies: Small businesses often struggle to reach their target audience and compete with larger competitors due to limited marketing budgets and resources. However, there are several solutions and ways of improvement that can help small businesses overcome this challenge: Focus on targeted marketing strategies: Instead of trying to reach a broad audience, small businesses should focus on targeted marketing strategies. This includes identifying their target market and tailoring marketing messages and channels to reach that specific audience. Social media advertising, content marketing, and local partnerships can be effective strategies for reaching a targeted audience without requiring a large marketing budget.

Utilize analytics tools: Small businesses should utilize analytics tools to measure the effectiveness of their marketing campaigns. By analyzing data and metrics, businesses can gain insights into customer behavior, preferences, and the performance of different marketing channels. This data-driven approach allows small businesses to make informed decisions and optimize their marketing efforts for better results. Leverage customer reviews and testimonials: Customer reviews and testimonials play a crucial role in building trust and credibility for small businesses. Encouraging satisfied customers to leave reviews or testimonials can help attract new customers and differentiate the business from competitors.

Operational inefficiencies: As small businesses grow, operational inefficiencies can arise due to outdated systems, lack of automation, and poor workflow management. However, investing in technological solutions, streamlining processes, and improving workflow management can help overcome this challenge. Here are some solutions and ways of improvement: Invest in technology solutions: Small businesses should invest in technology solutions that can improve efficiency and productivity. Customer relationship management (CRM) software can help manage customer interactions and improve customer service. Project management tools can streamline project workflows and enhance collaboration among team members. Inventory management systems can optimize inventory levels, reduce waste, and improve supply chain management.

Streamline processes and workflows: Small businesses should regularly review their processes and workflows to identify areas for improvement. By eliminating unnecessary steps, automating repetitive tasks, and standardizing processes, small businesses can improve efficiency and reduce operational costs. Process mapping and workflow analysis can help identify bottlenecks or areas where improvements can be made. Embrace continuous improvement: Small businesses should embrace a culture of continuous improvement. Encouraging employees to identify areas for improvement and providing opportunities for feedback and suggestions can lead to innovative solutions and increased efficiency. Regular performance evaluations and monitoring key performance indicators (KPIs) can help track progress and identify areas that need further improvement.

Scalability challenges: Small businesses may struggle to scale their operations effectively without disrupting existing processes or compromising quality. However, developing a scalable business model and continuously monitoring and adapting the business model can help overcome this challenge. Here are some solutions and ways of improvement:

Develop a scalable business model: Small businesses should focus on standardization, automation, and outsourcing non-core functions to develop a scalable business model. By standardizing processes and workflows, small businesses can ensure consistency and efficiency as they grow. Automation can help streamline repetitive tasks and reduce the need for manual intervention. Outsourcing non-core functions such as accounting, IT support, or marketing can free up internal resources and allow the business to focus on core competencies. Continuously monitor and adapt the business model: Small businesses should continuously monitor market trends, customer preferences, and industry developments to ensure their business model remains relevant and adaptable. Regularly reviewing and updating the business plan, financial projections,

Lack of market differentiation: Small businesses often face intense competition from larger players in the market, making it difficult to differentiate their products or services. However, by identifying a unique selling proposition (USP) and emphasizing personalized customer experiences, niche markets, or specialized expertise, small businesses can overcome this challenge. Here are some solutions and ways of improvement: Identify a unique selling proposition (USP): Small businesses should identify a USP that sets them apart from competitors. This could be a unique feature or benefit of the product or service, a specialized expertise or skill set, or a personalized customer experience. By clearly communicating the USP to customers, small businesses can attract customers who value what makes them unique.

Emphasize personalized customer experiences: Small businesses can differentiate themselves by providing personalized customer experiences. This can include offering tailored products or services, providing exceptional customer service, or going above and beyond to meet customer needs. Building strong relationships with customers and understanding their preferences and pain points can help small businesses create a loyal customer base.Target niche markets: Instead of trying to compete with larger competitors in saturated markets, small businesses can target niche markets where they can provide specialized products or services. By focusing on a specific customer segment or industry, small businesses can build a reputation as experts in that field and attract customers who value their expertise.

Limited access to technology and innovation: Small businesses may lag behind in adopting new technologies and innovative practices due to cost constraints or lack of awareness. However, by staying updated with industry trends, investing in technology that improves efficiency and enhances customer experiences, and seeking partnerships or collaborations with technology providers or industry experts, small businesses can overcome this challenge. Here are some solutions and ways of improvement:

Stay updated with industry trends: Small businesses should actively stay updated with industry trends and developments. This can be done through attending industry conferences, subscribing to industry newsletters or publications, or participating in industry-specific forums or associations. By staying informed about emerging technologies and innovative practices, small businesses can identify opportunities for improvement and growth. Invest in technology that improves efficiency: Small businesses should carefully assess their operational needs and invest in technology solutions that can improve efficiency and productivity. This could include adopting cloud-based software solutions that streamline processes, implementing e-commerce platforms to expand online sales channels,

Seek partnerships or collaborations: Small businesses can overcome limited access to technology and innovation by seeking partnerships or collaborations with technology providers or industry experts. This could involve partnering with a technology company to develop customized solutions, collaborating with universities or research institutions to access cutting-edge research or expertise, or joining industry networks or clusters that promote collaboration and knowledge sharing.

Expanding a small business can be challenging due to various obstacles that hinder growth and success. However, by proactively addressing these challenges and implementing the solutions and ways of improvement discussed in this article, small businesses can overcome barriers to expansion. Limited financial resources can be addressed by exploring alternative financing options and developing a detailed business plan. Lack of skilled workforce can be mitigated by investing in employee training and development programs and fostering a positive work culture. Ineffective marketing strategies can be improved through targeted marketing strategies, analytics tools, and leveraging customer reviews. Operational inefficiencies can be addressed through technological solutions, streamlined processes, and continuous improvement. Scalability challenges can be overcome by developing a scalable business model and continuously monitoring and adapting the business model. Lack of market differentiation can be addressed by identifying a unique selling proposition and emphasizing personalized customer experiences or targeting niche markets. Limited access to technology and innovation can be overcome by staying updated with industry trends, investing in technology, and seeking partnerships or collaborations. By being proactive, adaptable, and continuously seeking improvement, small businesses can successfully expand and thrive in a competitive market. Lack of market differentiation can be addressed by identifying a unique selling proposition and emphasizing personalized customer experiences or targeting niche markets. Limited access to technology and innovation can be overcome by staying updated with industry trends, investing in technology, and seeking partnerships or collaborations. By being proactive, adaptable, and continuously seeking improvement, small businesses can successfully expand and thrive in a competitive market. Lack of market differentiation can be addressed by identifying a unique selling proposition and emphasizing personalized customer experiences or targeting niche markets. Limited access to technology and innovation can be overcome by staying updated with industry trends, investing in technology, and seeking partnerships or collaborations. By being proactive, adaptable, and continuously seeking improvement, small businesses can successfully expand and thrive in a competitive market. investing in technology, and seeking partnerships or collaborations. By being proactive, adaptable, and continuously seeking improvement, small businesses can successfully expand and thrive in a competitive market. Lack of market differentiation can be addressed by identifying a unique selling proposition and emphasizing personalized customer experiences or targeting niche markets. Limited access to technology and innovation can be overcome by staying updated with industry trends, investing in technology, and seeking partnerships or collaborations. By being proactive, adaptable, and continuously seeking improvement, small businesses can successfully expand and thrive in a competitive market. investing in technology, and seeking partnerships or collaborations. By being proactive, adaptable, and continuously seeking improvement, small businesses can successfully expand and thrive in a competitive market. Lack of market differentiation can be addressed by identifying a unique selling proposition and emphasizing personalized customer experiences or targeting niche markets. Limited access to technology and innovation can be overcome by staying updated with industry trends, investing in technology, and seeking partnerships or collaborations. By being proactive, adaptable, and continuously seeking improvement, small businesses can successfully expand and thrive in a competitive market. small businesses can successfully expand and thrive in a competitive market. Lack of market differentiation can be addressed by identifying a unique selling proposition and emphasizing personalized customer experiences or targeting niche markets. Limited access to technology and innovation can be overcome by staying updated with industry trends, investing in technology, and seeking partnerships or collaborations. By being proactive, adaptable, and continuously seeking improvement, small businesses can successfully expand and thrive in a competitive market. small businesses can successfully expand and thrive in a competitive market. Lack of market differentiation can be addressed by identifying a unique selling proposition and emphasizing personalized customer experiences or targeting niche markets. Limited access to technology and innovation can be overcome by staying updated with industry trends, investing in technology, and seeking partnerships or collaborations. By being proactive, adaptable, and continuously seeking improvement, small businesses can successfully expand and thrive in a competitive market. Limited access to technology and innovation can be overcome by staying updated with industry trends, investing in technology, and seeking partnerships or collaborations. By being proactive, adaptable, and continuously seeking improvement, small businesses can successfully expand and thrive in a competitive market. Limited access to technology and innovation can be overcome by staying updated with industry trends, investing in technology, and seeking partnerships or collaborations. By being proactive, adaptable, and continuously seeking improvement, small businesses can successfully expand and thrive in a competitive market.

CHAPTER II. The economic costs of the Russia-Ukraine conflict.

This abstract takes a comprehensive look at the economic consequences of the Russia-Ukraine conflict that began in 2022. It includes a sharp decline in economic growth in Ukraine, including disruptions in trade and investment, contraction in key industries, inflation, currency depreciation and budget deficits. It also discusses the serious economic costs for Russia, such as limited access to global financial markets and technology due to international sanctions, as well as the impact of falling oil prices on its energy-dependent economy. The topic emphasizes the loss of human capital, displacement of people, and diversion of resources from productive investment and social welfare programs in both countries. Besides, it recognizes the negative consequences of the EU as a major trading partner.

According to global econometric analysis, after the war in Russia and Ukraine, we can see the impact on the total GDP. It is expected that the level of GDP will decrease by 1 percent, and as a result, the global GDP may decrease by 1 trillion dollars.

We know that Russia and Ukraine are the main exporters in many fields, such as titanium, wheat, palladium, corn and gold, and are the leaders in the gas market. many countries are suffering, but European countries are suffering more. Due to the sanctions imposed on European and G7 countries,

European countries are wearing less clothes, especially in oil and gas networks, the state is paying a lot of money at the expense of the state, and it is becoming more expensive for these countries. But these restrictions do not limit Russia's GDP. indicators are expected to fall from 1.5 percent to 2.5 percent, and it is expected that by 2023, the inflation rate in Russia will exceed 20 percent.

Ukraine is not an important trade partner for any major economy. But Russia is an important strategic partner for the European Union, Great Britain and some Asian countries. China, the USA, Germany, Italy, and France are Russia's main import partners. According to the International Monetary Fund (IMF), in 2022 Russia's share of world GDP was expected to be 1.6 percent, while Ukraine's economic output was predicted to be 0.2 percent of world output. Although Russia and Ukraine do not have a very large share in the world market and economy, they are leaders in some areas, and the failure or slowing down of these areas will have a great impact on other areas, and these areas will increase the position of these countries in the field of energy and food, and they will have a great power in these areas in the world economy. An example of this is the disruption of industrial production in European countries and the rise in food prices due to the failure of these industries. And many scientists call it stronger than an infectious disease. This conflict affects Asian countries as well, because Russia is increasing the demand in Asian countries, and this has a direct impact on the increase in food prices in

Asian countries. In agriculture, which is a high and necessary sector in world trade, these 2 countries are important links, that is, these 2 countries export a quarter of the world's wheat exports. In addition, there are significant exports of corn and other large grains, with Ukraine and Russia accounting for almost a fifth of world exports. 80% of sunflower oil exports go to Russia and Ukraine. Due to sanctions and logistical problems,

Not only in food, but also in technology and industry, for example, Russia is a major producer of palladium, which is used in engine exhausts to reduce emissions, where it accounts for 40 percent of global mine production and about 10 percent of global platinum supply. 10 percent is produced. The global supply of titanium sponge used in airplanes produces and provides 15%. And these indicators cause shortages in the automotive, aircraft and logistics sectors due to sanctions and economic policies, and therefore other suppliers in the market raise prices and gradually reduce the cost of providing services. There may be interruptions and delays in car prices and related areas.

According to our scientists, Russia's influence on the world economy is small, but they are wrong in this matter, because the Russian state is the main exporter of oil and gas, and if these imposed sanctions continue or increase this year, it will greatly affect the black gold market and increase its price. The increase in the price of oil will lead to the increase in the value of many sectors, and it is expected that many sectors will break.

We have now seen Brent oil prices rise above $100 per barrel, the highest level since 2014. Crude oil changes account for about 40 percent of fuel price changes in the US, but much less in Europe. The tax rate is significantly higher. In our simulation, we assume that oil prices will rise to $40 per barrel, an increase that averages 7.1 percent in 2022 and 3.3 percent in 2023, compared with 4.6 percent and 2.5 percent in the February forecast for US inflation, respectively. will lead to 5 percent. In the February forecast in the euro area, inflation is expected to be 5.5 percent in 2022 and 2.1 percent in 2023, compared to forecasts of 3.1 percent in 2022 and 1.3 percent in 2023.

Economic sanctions against Russia. More than 80 percent of Russia's daily foreign exchange transactions and half of its trade are in US dollars. And for this reason, the Russian state is currently trying to reduce the US dollar and lower its reputation, as we can see from the fact that Russia has announced that it will sell oil and gas only for Russian rubles. European Union, USA, Canada, UK, Japan and Australia banks, wealthy individuals have been targeted, Russia's top oligarchs have been affected by sanctions on their luxury goods or businesses, and Germany has suspended a major Russian gas pipeline project. The Russian central bank's foreign reserves were frozen and its banks restricted from using the SWIFT international payment system, but Europe shrugged off the sanctions for little benefit, allowing energy transactions and gas payments. The sanctions, which are tougher than those imposed in 2014 following Russia's annexation of Crimea, were included in the first sanctions document aimed at blocking certain Russian state-owned banks from selling their debt in the US, European and Japanese markets.

The European countries are facing the economic decline of Russia and the economic decline of this country, ie these imposed sanctions will lead to a decrease in prices in other sectors except the energy sector. The ban on the sale of semiconductor microchips to the Russian corporations, these sectors will export 6.25 million dollars of Russian imports to the Russian defense and aerospace sector. According to forecasts, if these sanctions are not removed through third countries and trade barriers remain, it is expected that Russian imports will decrease by 30%.

These sanctions have a strong impact on Europe as well. The increase in energy prices causes inflation to rise. For example, in the US, the relative importance of energy in the CPI is 7.3 percent, with energy goods such as fuel accounting for 4 percent and energy services such as electricity and gas pipelines accounting for 3.3 percent. In Great Britain, electricity, gas and other fuels account for 3.3% of the CPI, and fuel and lubricants account for another 2.7%. These restrictions may have little effect on China or the USA, and these countries can satisfy the demand in their countries without importing at all. And China is using this policy to buy Russia's oil and gas products at cheap prices, and it is benefiting from this shortage. In these economic restrictions, many European countries are at a loss because the increase in energy prices or energy shortages will affect the cost of living. One part of the European countries' oil imports and half of the natural gas imports are bought from Russia. The European Union receives 60% of its energy demand from other countries. Eastern European countries are completely dependent on energy imports, and Germany is 40% dependent on Russian gas, which shows that these countries are dependent on Russian energy. It is possible to get out of this by going green energy system, but it is a big investment and takes more time. Eastern European countries are completely dependent on energy imports, and Germany is 40% dependent on Russian gas, which shows that these countries are dependent on Russian energy. It is possible to get out of this by going green energy system, but it is a big investment and takes more time. Eastern European countries are completely dependent on energy imports, and Germany is 40% dependent on Russian gas, which shows that these countries are dependent on Russian energy. It is possible to get out of this by going green energy system, but it is a big investment and takes more time.

One of the biggest problems is the immigration problem. According to the forecasts of European scientists, more than 4 million refugees may enter the European Union, and this may be a burden for countries such as Poland, which is close to it, and many problems may arise there. This is mainly due to G For Western Europe, it poses serious problems in terms of housing, public finances, employment and possible social tensions. The OECD estimated in 2017 that the cost of an asylum seeker's first year was around €10,000. Asylum seekers cost Germany more than €20 billion in 2016 (Kroet, 2017). In 2015, the financial costs of asylum seekers in Germany amounted to about 0.5% of GDP, in Sweden, it was about 1.35% of GDP; In Austria, however, spending was three-quarters of a percentage point of GDP in 2017 and 2018 (OECD, 2017). According to European economists, first aid is not the main problem for the Ukrainians, they should allocate sufficient funds for their defense, and in this case, it is necessary to increase the potential of the country. This is because China has risen much more since this war and continues to rise. He is showing that he has to spend a lot of money on his small military force. But since little Europe is suffering in this war, this is increasing the pressure. For example, particularly crisis-hit NATO EU countries, eg Germany increased military spending and finally bowed to US pressure to bring defense spending closer to 2 percent of GDP. Defense spending in NATO is likely to increase over the next few years: it will amount to 0.5 percent of GDP over two years, which is equivalent to an increase in defense spending in Western Europe of about 30 percent. here, most countries do not think that they will be able to achieve NATO's goal of spending 2% of GDP, and it is emphasized that 1.6% is needed on average. In addition to NATO, Sweden, Finland and several Eastern European countries have also begun to significantly increase defense spending in response to the Russia-Ukraine crisis, and more of this GDP is being directed to defense and military sectors. Defense spending in NATO is likely to increase over the next few years: it will amount to 0.5 percent of GDP over two years, which is equivalent to an increase in defense spending in Western Europe of about 30 percent. here, most countries do not think that they will be able to achieve NATO's goal of spending 2% of GDP, and it is emphasized that 1. 6% is needed on average. In addition to NATO, Sweden, Finland and several Eastern European countries have also begun to significantly increase defense spending in response to the Russia-Ukraine crisis, and more of this GDP is being directed to defense and military sectors. Defense spending in NATO is likely to increase over the next few years: it will amount to 0.5 percent of GDP over two years, which is equivalent to an increase in defense spending in Western Europe of about 30 percent. here, most countries do not think that they will be able to achieve NATO's goal of spending 2% of GDP, and it is emphasized that 1.6% is needed on average. In addition to NATO, Sweden, Finland and several Eastern European countries have also begun to significantly increase defense spending in response to the Russia-Ukraine crisis, and more of this GDP is being directed to defense and military sectors. here, most countries do not think that they will be able to achieve NATO's goal of spending 2% of GDP, and it is emphasized that 1.6% is needed on average. In addition to NATO, Sweden, Finland and several Eastern European countries have also begun to significantly increase defense spending in response to the Russia-Ukraine crisis, and more of this GDP is being directed to defense and military sectors. here, most countries do not think that they will be able to achieve

NATO's goal of spending 2% of GDP, and it is emphasized that 1.6% is needed on average. In addition to NATO, Sweden, Finland and several Eastern European countries have also begun to significantly increase defense spending in response to the Russia-Ukraine crisis,

In Russia, during this conflict, inflation may rise, and this inflation may lead to crisis and political problems. Both Russia and Russia may benefit from the energy crisis, because it is possible to fill the existing deficit due to the increase in oil and gas prices, because of this crisis, countries like China, India and Turkey even if you buy it, it can reduce the crisis. Or, by improving the relations with 3 countries, they can enter the market and buy a few products, thereby keeping the problems in other fields for a short time.

During the crisis, the financial markets are experiencing sharp disruptions and negative effects, especially the stock markets and cryptocurrency markets are experiencing significant declines. And the Russian stock markets are experiencing huge losses, as the shares of many Russian giant companies have fallen significantly, and the business performance in Russia is very low. is in a bad situation and small business owners are suffering a lot from this crisis. The giant campaigns are attracting a lot of money, and the Russian government is covering this with difficulty, but its position in the stock market is not deteriorating day by day. No bonds and promissory notes of the Russian government are allowed to work on the market. The next problem is that many investors are withdrawing their assets from Russia, and because of this, the amount of money coming from taxes is decreasing. New investors are not investing in Russian campaigns. The unprecedented move by Russia's central bank is aimed at limiting currency availability, which could crowd out imports, while increasing demand for liquidity, draining funds from banks and restricting credit as a potential source of risk in the domestic banking system. is being watched. These effects are difficult to quantify, but European economists point to downside risks to Russia's growth outlook, while inflation is on the upside. The ruble is expected to fall by up to 70% this year as a result of high Russian inflation and the risk of over 20%. The unprecedented move by Russia's central bank is aimed at limiting currency availability, which could crowd out imports, while increasing demand for liquidity, draining funds from banks and restricting credit as a potential source of risk in the domestic banking system. is being watched. These effects are difficult to quantify, but European economists point to downside risks to Russia's growth outlook, while inflation is on the upside. The ruble is expected to fall by up to 70% this year as a result of high Russian inflation and the risk of over 20%. The unprecedented move by Russia's central bank is aimed at limiting currency availability, which could crowd out imports, while increasing demand for liquidity, draining funds from banks and restricting credit as a potential source of risk in the domestic banking system. is being watched. These effects are difficult to quantify, but European economists point to downside risks to Russia's growth outlook, while inflation is on the upside. The ruble is expected to fall by up to 70% this year as a result of high Russian inflation and the risk of over 20%. credit is seen as a source of potential risk in a restrictive local banking system that drains funds from banks. These effects are difficult to quantify, but European economists point to downside risks to Russia's growth outlook, while inflation is on the upside. The ruble is expected to fall by up to 70% this year as a result of high Russian inflation and the risk of over 20%. credit is seen as a source of potential risk in a restrictive local banking system that drains funds from banks. These effects are difficult to quantify, but European economists point to downside risks to Russia's growth outlook, while inflation is on the upside.

The war between Russia and Ukraine had a significant impact on the world economy and created problems for many countries. But at this time, energy exporters are much more profitable. During this time, the sharp rise in prices caused many problems. Since the beginning of the war, some countries have strengthened their political power, and some countries are losing, because of the denial of European countries or the political position of China and Turkey. we can see that it helped the financial situation, but according to the current reports, the damage in Ukraine is in the amount of 200 billion dollars, and in Russia, it is said that the damage is in the amount of 300 billion dollars.

Used resources

1 AHDB. (n.d.). Do wheat prices matter for bread? Grain Market Daily | AHDB. Retrieved February 25, 2022, from https://ahdb.org.uk/news/do-wheat-prices-matter-for-bread

2 Anstey, C. (2022, February 25). Three Ways the Ukraine Crisis May Rattle the World Economy.

3 Bloomberg.Com. https://www.bloomberg.com/news/newsletters/2022-02-25/globaleconomy-latest-three-ways-ukraine-crisis-hurts-world-economy

4 Associated Press. (2022, February 26). Ukraine crisis: UNHCR predicts 4 million will flee to neighboring countries. Business Standard India. https://www.businessstandard.com/article/international/ukraine-crisis-unhcr-predicts-4-mn-will-flee-toneighbouring-countries-122022600772_1.html

5 d'Albis, H., Boubtane, E., & Coulibaly, D. (n.d.). Macroeconomic evidence suggests that asylum seekers are not a "burden" for Western European countries. Science Advances, 4(6), eaaq0883. https://doi.org/10.1126/sciadv.aaq0883

6 ECB, EC (2022). Economic Bulletin Issue 1, 2022. https://www.ecb.europa.eu//pub/economicbulletin/html/eb202201.en.html

7Economist, The. (2022, January 29). How will Europe cope if Russia cuts off its gas? https://www.economist.com/europe/2022/01/29/how-will-europe-cope-if-russia-cutsoff-its-gas

Kroet, C. (2017, January 27). Refugee crisis cost Germany over €20 billion in 2016. POLITICO. https://www.politico.eu/article/refugee-crisis-cost-germany-over-e20-billion-in-2016/

8Lejeune, T. (2022, February 26). Europe braces for wave of Ukrainian refugees [Text]. TheHill. https://thehill.com/policy/international/595918-europe-braces-for-wave-of-ukrainianrefugees

9Macchiarelli, C., & B. Naisbitt; J. Boshoff, I. Hurst, I. Liadze, I, X. Mao, P. Sánchez Juanino, C.

10Thamotheram "Global Economic Outlook - Inflation: Central Bank on It" (2022), National Institute Economic Review, 259, Winter.

11Mearsheimer, JJ (2019). Bound to Fail: The Rise and Fall of the Liberal International Order. International Security, 43(4), 7–50. https://doi.org/10.1162/isec_a_00342

2.1 Economic implications of the Russia-Ukraine conflict on EU economic policy, including fiscal support and monetary monitoring.

Discusses the economic consequences of the Russia-Ukraine conflict on the economic policy of the European Union. This highlights the need for fiscal support and monetary monitoring to mitigate the economic damage caused by the conflict. The conflict has led to reduced economic growth, trade disruptions, investment disruptions, sector contraction, inflation, currency depreciation, fiscal deficits, restricted access to financial markets and technology, and international sanctions. In addition, falling oil prices and an energy-dependent economy have exacerbated economic problems. Conflict has also led to the loss of human capital, displacement of people and loss of resources. To address these challenges, the EU must focus on restoring stability, resolving conflicts and promoting long-term recovery.

According to EU trade statistics, exports of goods to Russia amounted to 89 billion euros in 2021. If they are stopped, the biggest estimate is that, among other things, the aggregate demand for EU goods will fall by 0.6% of 2019 GDP. will bring. A 50 percent reduction in goods exports to Russia would reduce GDP by 0.3 percent. It is mentioned without taking into account the aggregate demand. Three thirds of all foreign investments made in Russia go to the European Union. In numbers, this means more than 300 billion euros. This outflow of money will significantly affect the Russian financial system and banks.

The global financial crisis of 2008 showed that if two financial banks go bankrupt, it will affect the next one, which will affect all financial countries, and the end result will worsen the economic situation of this country. For example, all Russian bank branches in the European Union have been closed, and this will have a significant impact on banks.

There are also migration problems. In April, 4.6 million people arrived from abroad, and before that, 7.1 million people were displaced, most of them women and children. A large amount of money costs from 9,000 to 25,000 euros per person per year. Even if we consider the average cost of 10,000 euros per person per year, this is a very large amount. As of April, 50 billion euros per year for 5 million refugees or 0.35% of the GDP of the European Union will come from abroad.

Russia and Ukraine are the main producers of wheat in the food industry, and their share in exports is also high. Russia and Ukraine export 23% of wheat in the world market. If we look at the bad relations of the European Union with Russia, even if we can get wheat from them, it will be difficult due to logistical problems. .In Ukraine, structures are falling apart and there is war in many cities, and if we look at the problems of delivery to other cities, there is a high probability of a shortage of wheat products by 2023.

The main problem for Europe now is the problem of heat sources, because it receives oil, gas and coal from Russia. 24 percent, mainly imported) and coal (12 percent, primarily imported). Russia has been the main supplier of coal, oil and gas for many years.

Yes, because of the sanctions in the energy sector, Russia's profits will not decrease, but if it stops trading with the West, it does not mean that it will not be able to sell at all. But the countries of the European Union are trying to get these products from other places, because they still have logistics or pipelines with the Arab countries, so this will cause a lot of damage to Europe.

In addition to these opinions, there are uncertainties regarding the future oil, gas, and coal food products of European countries due to the decision of Russia and the sanctions imposed by the European Union and the influence of the G7 countries. In Europe, gas prices will double and reach 200 euros per MWh. These resources are expected to increase by 25% compared to their pre-war price due to rationing decisions and EU sanctions.

The prices of earlier goods have increased many times and this has affected the purchasing power of people. Looking at oil prices alone: Brent rose from $10.27 a barrel in February 1999 to $133 in July 2008, then from $40 in December 2008 to $123 in April 2011. It was above $100 until August 2014. Adjusted for inflation since 2014, $100 back then is worth $120 today, so the current real price of oil has not yet reached historical records. As a result, economists have a good understanding of the effect of rising commodity prices on the economy, and accordingly, the forecasts differ, and these forecasts are somewhat closer to reality.

In addition to what we have already said, these numbers will immediately affect inflation. It is clear that the scope of influence will be much higher. Because in 2021, in European countries, electricity, transport and heating fuel will account for 9.6% of personal consumption expenses, and 15.7% for food consumption. came out.

For example, take 10 percent for the share of energy in private consumption and assume a 50 percent transition. The direct effect of an assumed 25 percent increase in prices is thus 25 percent × 0.1 × 0.5 = 1.25 percent. For food, let's assume 15 percent share, 10 percent growth, and 0.5 percent transition. The effect is 10 percent × 0.15 × 0.5 = 0.75 percent. This implies an increase in the price of the consumer basket by the first 2 percent. The responses of firms and workers to these effects.

Whether the economy produces these goods or imports them affects the dynamics of inflation.

Gas markets have also pulled back from February's price hikes, but remain high. For example, the average percentage increase in the price of gas for the European Union is the same as that of oil, about 25 percent. In 2021, gas imports (from Russia and elsewhere) amounted to 170 billion euros. This means a real income reduction for the EU of 170 × 0.25 ÿ 42 billion euros, or 0.3% of 2019 GDP.

Now, what will these situations look like in monetary policy and fiscal policy? Can these policies protect the population from such price changes in the short term? According to our estimates, the average increase in consumer prices, including wages, is 2% external. poor and resource-poor countries suffer a lot, for example, Slovakia, where the real income decline is 2-fold. Saving households from this situation and alleviating this economic problem is still being discussed, and so far, solutions are given in 3 headings.

Temporary reduction of energy taxes. 1st aid is comprehensive subsidies, for example, reducing energy taxes, because in some European countries these taxes are very high. For example, France introduced a 1-year cut in electricity taxes in February (8 billion euros or 0.3% of GDP) and a 4-month gasoline tax cut of 15 cents per liter on April 1. The estimated cost is 2.2 billion euros, which is about 0.1% of GDP. This subsidy will be provided as a stopgap until a more targeted system is introduced in early summer. This is a very visible, political advantage. Temporary rebates similar to excise duty have been introduced in other countries, notably

One-time money transfers. The main option for this is to make transfers, because this will greatly help with the consumption of food, gas and oil. For example, Germany introduced a universal lump sum payment (Energiepreis-Pauschale) on March 23 of €300 per person plus child allowance. Last year, France introduced a 100-euro compensatory inflation rate to people earning no more than 2,000 euros a month, amounting to 3.8 billion euros, or about 0.2 percent of GDP, automatically. Such measures are unlikely to affect market prices. For food, oil and gas (only to the extent that additional income is spent on these).

Regulation of prices. For example, separating the price of electricity from the marginal price. That is, lowering the price of electricity in the market and removing the marginal costs from it, the campaign requires the government to reduce the costs for the child. Spain has been particularly vocal in its criticism of the inflationary effects of electricity prices, and in March it received EU approval to temporarily cut the Iberian Peninsula from the EU electricity market. France has asked the country's main electricity company to limit price increases to 4 percent for 2022 and meet demand at that price.

There are 2 arguments against subsidies. First of all, it increases the demand for energy, and because of this, it causes the price of energy to rise and keep it rising. The change in consumer prices also affects market prices, so it causes problems if it is used in any country or if it has a high share in the global market. We know that all the countries of the European Union if this is implemented, the energy sources in the global market will quickly increase, and due to the high demand, it will not be a floating line, but only an increasing line. Type 2 will also affect Europe's relations with Russia in the future, and discounts or subsidies in the small market will have a bad effect on domestic gas producers.

What will be the effect of the allocation of additional aid or debt in the fiscal policy on the monetary policy of the EU? The financial costs are increasing now because of this aggression of Russia, the European Union is increasing its defense purchases, and this is a small cost, but the help of weapons to Ukraine Was it cheap to give, did it cost them a lot of money to finance the refugees, and the highest costs are the problems in the energy system. The European Union does not say that it should not exceed 2% of GDP, but this should not be because the costs are high. Fiscal and monetary policy are closely related. Now central banks are suffering from these problems and private companies are demanding more. If it can increase the money supply and decrease the supply, then the central bank wins. If this is beneficial to Russia, it will not increase the emission. But if inflation is not curbed by monetary policy, the countries will suffer a lot.

In conclusion, the war in Ukraine was a big blow for Europe. Because taking care of refugees, increasing the defense and military capacity, reducing energy resources, increasing the price of food products, disruptions in the gas and oil market, and the labor market and the decrease in demand have led to a worse situation.

Energy prices may rise much higher than they have been, or return to pre-war levels. That is, real income losses and inflationary pressures may be much larger than currently projected, or instead may be less of a problem. This leads to our final conclusion. Fiscal and monetary policy should be flexible, consisting of measures that are easy to change as needed.

References.

Bachmann, R., D. Baqaee, C. Bayer, M. Kuhn, A. Löschel, B. Moll, A. Peichl, K. Pittel, andM. Schularick. 2022. What if? The Economic Effects for Germany of a Stop of Energy Imports from Russia. ECONtribute Policy Brief 028, March 7, https://www.econtributede/RePEc/ajk/ajkpbs/ECONtribute_PB_028_2022.pdf.

Baqaee, D., and B. Moll. 2022. What if Germany is cut off from Russian oil and gas? Marcus Academy, April 7, https://bcf.princeton.edu/events/david-baquee-and-ben-moll-onwhat-if-germany-is-cut-off-from-russian-oil-and-gas/ .

Blanchard, Olivier, and Jordi Galí. 2007. Real wage rigidities and the New Keynesian model. Journal of Money, Credit, and Banking 39: 35–65.

Blanchard, Olivier. 2023. Fiscal policy under low interest rates. Forthcoming. MIT Press. Pre-publication version available at https://fiscal-policy-under-low-interestrates.pubpub.org/.

Bown, Chad P. 2022. Russia's war on Ukraine: A sanctions timeline. PIIE RealTime Economic Issues Watch, April 14, https://www.piie.com/blogs/realtime-economic-issues-watch/russias-war-ukraine-sanctions-timeline.

BP. 2021. Statistical Review of World Energy. London.

Darvas, Zsolt. 2022. Bold European Union action is needed to support Ukrainian refugees. Bruegel blog, April 6, https://www.bruegel.org/2022/04/bold-european-union-actionis-needed-to-support-ukrainian-refugees .

CHAPTER III. The main problems faced by business entities operating in the territory of Uzbekistan.

Bureaucratic and administrative barriers, lack of available funds, lack of qualified personnel, underdeveloped infrastructure and corruption - all this can make business development difficult and create unequal conditions for competition. They require attention and appropriate measures to facilitate business activities in the country.

In addition, we will consider possible solutions and development directions to help overcome these problems. Simplification of bureaucratic procedures, reduction of tax burden, creation of a more favorable legal and investment environment, support of innovation and development of education - all this helps to attract investments, increase entrepreneurial activity and stimulate economic growth.

As a result, the development and implementation of appropriate strategies and policies in Uzbekistan will help to eliminate the problems faced by economic entities, create a favorable environment for the development of entrepreneurship and attracting investments.

Business entities in the territory of Uzbekistan may face various problems. Some of the main problems they may face are:

Tax System: The complexity of the tax system and high tax rates can have a negative impact on business. Simplification of tax procedures, reduction of tax burden and a more transparent system of taxation can stimulate business activities and attract more investments.

Bureaucratic barriers: Uzbekistan still has a complex and multi-layered regulatory system, which can make it difficult to register a business, obtain licenses, permits and other documents. Bureaucratic inefficiencies can lead to delays and additional costs for entrepreneurs.

Legal system and protection of property rights: It is important to develop and enforce an effective legal system that ensures protection of property rights and contractual obligations. This helps to reduce risks and increase the confidence of investors and entrepreneurs.

Development of international relations: Uzbekistan can benefit from the development of international economic relations and trade. Increasing the level of exports and attracting foreign investments will help to diversify the economy and expand business opportunities.

Innovation and technology development: supporting innovation and technology development play an important role in the sustainable development of business. Creating special programs and incentives for research and development, as well as promoting the introduction of new technologies, will help to increase the competitiveness of enterprises and attract investments.

Corruption: Corruption remains a significant problem in Uzbekistan. Some entrepreneurs may face demands for bribes or other illegal payments to obtain permits or speed up processes. This can create unfavorable business conditions and increase costs.

Inadequate financing: many business entities may face the problem of obtaining credit and financing to expand or develop their business. The banking system may be underdeveloped or limited, which makes it difficult to get the necessary funds.

Infrastructural underdevelopment: Infrastructure may be underdeveloped in a number of regions of Uzbekistan. Problems with the availability of quality roads, electricity supply, water supply and telecommunications can complicate business processes and increase costs for entrepreneurs.

Lack of skilled workers: Some industries and regions may lack skilled workers or professionals. This can make business development difficult and increase the need for employee training.

Tax and Regulatory Environment: The complexity of tax law and the uncertainty of its interpretation can also be a problem for business entities.

High competition: There may be high competition in a number of sectors in Uzbekistan, especially in the retail and service sectors. This can cause problems for small and medium-sized enterprises, which are struggling to compete with the big players.

Change in legislation: Unpredictable changes in legislation can create uncertainty for entrepreneurs and make it difficult to plan long-term strategies. The constant need to adapt to new regulations can be difficult for a business.

It should be noted that Uzbekistan is actively working on reforming and improving the business environment. Many of these issues are already being addressed by the government and steps are being taken to remove barriers and create a favorable business environment.

Lack of available markets and diversification: opportunities to export and expand business in international markets may be limited. Some businesses may struggle to find new markets for their products or services, making it difficult for them to grow and diversify.

Underdeveloped digital infrastructure: Inadequate digital infrastructure can make it difficult for businesses to use modern technology and digital tools. This can limit the efficiency and competitiveness of enterprises.

Macroeconomic instability: fluctuations in macroeconomic conditions, including inflation, exchange rate fluctuations and other economic factors, can create uncertainty and risks for business. This can make it difficult to plan and make long-term decisions.

Lack of innovative activity: lack of innovation and limited opportunities for research and development of new technologies can reduce the competitiveness of economic entities. A lack of innovation can hinder the development and creation of new market opportunities.

Social and Cultural Constraints: Some industries or regions may have social or cultural constraints that make it difficult to develop certain business ideas or practices. This may include advertising restrictions, traditional prejudices or cultural norms.

These problems may differ depending on the industries, scale of enterprises and regional characteristics in Uzbekistan. However, the government and the business community are actively working to solve these problems and create a more favorable and supportive environment for business entities.

Simplify bureaucratic procedures: The government can take steps to simplify procedures for business registration, licenses and permits. The introduction of electronic systems and the reduction of paperwork will help reduce bureaucratic costs and speed up processes.

Anti-corruption: Implementation of transparency, ethical standards and zero tolerance for corruption is an important factor in creating a fair business environment. It is important to strengthen legal and penal mechanisms, conduct anti-corruption investigations and create complaint mechanisms so that entrepreneurs can operate safely.

Development of available financial instruments: Government can help develop the financial sector and create conditions for entrepreneurs to have wider access to credit and financing. This includes government support programs, loan guarantees, lower bank rates, and the development of alternative financing sources such as venture capital investments and crowdfunding.

Infrastructure investment: The government can prioritize investment in infrastructure development such as roads, power, water supply and telecommunications. Improvement of infrastructure helps to reduce costs of enterprises and creates good conditions for business development.

Development of education and vocational training: the field of education should be adapted to the needs of the labor market. Development of government vocational training programs

Encourage innovation and technological development: government can create incentives to promote innovation, research and development. This includes tax incentives, research and development grants, the creation of incubators and technology parks, and facilitating the transfer of technology from academia to business.

Support for small and medium-sized enterprises: special support programs may be provided to small and medium-sized enterprises, such as access to consulting services, training and education, and subsidies for opening new enterprises or expanding existing ones.

Development of international relations and trade: improving access to international markets and creating favorable conditions for exports will help enterprises to expand and diversify their business. The government can conclude trade agreements, develop infrastructure for exports, and assist in international marketing and promotion of goods.

Promoting Entrepreneurship: The government can implement promotional campaigns, activities and programs aimed at promoting entrepreneurship and developing entrepreneurial skills among youth and women. This may include educational programs, scholarships, competitions, and mentoring programs.

Communication with the business community: the government should support open and constructive communication with entrepreneurs and representatives of the business community. Establishing regular meetings, consultation sessions and feedback mechanisms will help the government understand the needs and challenges of business and take more effective measures to address them.

In conclusion, economic entities operating in the territory of Uzbekistan are facing several main problems. Bureaucratic and administrative barriers, lack of available funds, lack of qualified personnel, underdeveloped infrastructure and corruption are the main challenges for business in the country. Solving these problems may require government action in cooperation with entrepreneurs and investors. Creating a more convenient and transparent business environment, simplifying procedures and increasing financing opportunities, developing educational programs and improving infrastructure will help develop entrepreneurship and attract investments to Uzbekistan.

Used literature

Analysis of the development of small business activity in the Republic of Uzbekistan e conference zone 168-170.

https://lex.uz/ru/docs/-18942?ONDATE=21.04.2021

https://bojkhona.uz/oz/lists/view/118

Finance: finance of business entities

Book of analysis of the financial condition of economic entities, pages 78-90.

Financial resources of economic entities

3.1. The economic effect of monetary policy for the economy and its role in the economy.

Towards the end of the 20th century, we saw the unexpected strong and steady rise of new conservative waves in politics and economic theory. The main goals and views of politicians and macroeconomists began to be motivated by Keynes' views. 'began to change. For example, the trivial theorems of the new classical policy of Friedman monetarism or the equivalence models of David Ricardo, these views and all of these points to the independence of central banks, the need to cancel privatization and regulation, the need to stimulate supplies, and the need to change budget balances.

The political views of this period show the guilt of the state, i.e., giving up future benefits for current benefits, only looking at today and increasing the spheres of influence on inflation. For example, when the inflation started, it became a problem to hold and protect it with the available forces. And Keynes had only Keynes to blame for this confusion because he wanted to attack and change a sound financial system.

In the late 1970s, the increase in the natural rate of unemployment was blamed on the monetary credit and fiscal policy activists of the academy. However, in the late 1980s and early 1990s, the main forces were independent central banks and balanced budget policies. Keynesian views continued to be criticized, and these critics are still it's nice to stop. One of the main criticisms was his opinion that the society should be radically changed. Keynesians paid attention to the demand function in order to change their basic views or to respond to critics. And with this, he kept the problems for a short time, and when unemployment was high, the state labor exchange began to offer other low-paying jobs. But this was only a delay of the Great Depression.

One might think that the ideas that gave rise to all the opinions were clearly stated by Keynes or his followers to be clearly evaluated and judged, as mentioned above. was adopted as an omnibus concept involving active intervention. This is not surprising, because the supporters of Keynes themselves did not always see each other on this issue, that is, they were against each other. Especially in the 1960s, the policy of changing the profile of income distribution, extensive programs of public investment, it was easy to tell that the "left wing" who proposed progressive tax schemes and so on were the "right wing" Keynesians. Apart from their direct effects on welfare, they can also be said to be Keynesian because they are policies that encourage consumption and support aggregate demand. On the other hand, "right-wing" Keynesians have often described and stated that they seek income and employment stability without touching social structures and minimizing intervention.

Keynes said in his lecture: "In my opinion, regardless of the nature of the policy of the monetary authority, there is no single long-term position of equally true equilibrium" The need for such a specific concept of monetary economics is due to the following was: "It is a mistake to think that it is relatively easy to adapt the hypothetical conclusions of real wage economics to the real world of monetary economics."

From Keynes' views, it is possible to get the defining elements of the monetary economy. And many private entrepreneurs try to earn money without accumulating goods. Keynes does not rely on any monetary illusion. His arguments for why economic agents prefer the form of money are twofold. First, in Clower's Aphorisms, money buys goods and goods buy money, but goods do not buy goods. After that, the demand for money increases and gives money more preference than goods.

Secondly, "the money paid for the factors of production is kept more than the product for which they are paid for production" which gave preference to liquid forms. Keynes later argued that the most important challenge for classical economists was related to the role of money as an asset. This was because, according to Keynes, they failed to properly address the problem of uncertainty as opposed to calculable risk. This problem can be seen as a result of Keynesianism and the criticism of this theory. If the insurance system is not a good solution for such economic uncertainties, then it is necessary to develop other defense strategies. This is the main reason why money does not have a neutral characteristic in the economy. Its 2 basic functions affect the approaches in the economy. First, money is needed to demand goods or services. And the interesting thing is that money itself did not have much influence on long-term power or profit-making power. The main reason for this was that money was considered wealth at that time. And the interesting thing is that money itself did not have much influence on long-term power or profit-making power. The main reason for this was that money was considered wealth at that time. And the interesting thing is that money itself did not have much influence on long-term power or profit-making power. The main reason for this was that money was considered wealth at that time.

Money can compete with other assets only by its influence on long-term assets. In a private and uncertain world, we can see money as the safe haven of the rich. As Marx said long before Keynes, purchasing power is the general representative of social wealth, as opposed to specific forms of wealth represented by specific goods. Therefore, money "alleviates the anxiety" of wealth holders.

The influence of money on employment is higher because consumers save money instead of holding goods for future needs. Interest indicators are higher. Also, productive use of their money, investing money in some area, can keep it as wealth.

Consumers can save and accumulate money or goods as wealth in the monetary and credit economy. Money is considered an asset because it can be used as an intermediary to invest in other investments or to develop assets. And in the short term, money is a good asset and its liquidity is considered high.

A person will lose or profit because of his decisions, how can you say it can be done with monetary policy, that is, a person should see money as a way to wealth, not as wealth, yes, money is a good asset, but how money will develop or decline in the long term is very uncertain. . Therefore, it is necessary to invest the money in a place that will give you a good income quickly, holding it or keeping it for a year will make you profit, and if you don't keep it, you may lose money due to inflation. It also affects the monetary policy of the country. That is, you will increase your profit by buying additional work place or equipment, taking advantage of the money, and the child will be the reason to run it. This is known as the multiplier, a central element of Keynesian macroeconomics. This is a systemic flaw: money should be safe, allows for fixed prices and contracts; but such money becomes a powerful means of storing wealth, so attractive that under certain circumstances the demand for other types of assets, including fixed assets, can shrink to the point of extinction.

Keynes mentions the 2 worst aspects of capitalism in the chapter of the book "General Theory". Excessive concentration of income and the system's ability to ensure full employment and productive capacity of the working people. Keynes considered the 2nd problem to be the worst because it is necessary to reduce inequalities or to change them, and to them, that is, to people in general, he considered it a mistake that the work of one person cannot achieve anything by serving only one person, i.e. he does not get paid according to his work.

Keynes, like Schumpeter, did not consider complete equality to be the goal, because people's efforts, efficiency, Accumulation of various rewards and their valuing according to their risks and differences from others emphasized that using them and becoming rich depends on their will and effort. The problem is not that the income is accumulated, but that it is not concentrated enough to stimulate the enterprise, taking into account these factors. Even if a person works hard in the company, if he is the same as a normal worker, no promotion or advancement simply lowers the employee's motivation to work. In particular, be the cause of inheritance law, e.g. the concentration of wealth was largely independent of economic indicators. The tax system must be aimed at correcting these unjustified sources of inequality, since a uniform tax insists that the government must use fiscal policy effectively to answer the question of whether the poor should only act for the rich.

The main decisions of the government have a strong influence on the market balance, that is, in order to solve the problems in the system, the state should influence the market with its less systematic management and policies. From the information provided on the side, we can get the idea that private enterprises or agents manage a small company or a single neighborhood. And the state should ensure that economy and politics are taken together and they should be used in the right way.

Keynes emphasized that there are three possible solutions to these problems. First, the state can take direct responsibility for investment decisions. Second, the state can try to give special benefits to private investments in selected areas. may tend to exert an effect whereby private agents may be motivated to make riskier choices rather than accumulating liquid assets.

In short, Keynes believed that government intervention was necessary and that the state should rule the world as an arbiter.

Fiscal policy assumes that Keynesian theory can have a good effect on GDP through taxation and inflation. Fiscal policy is a tool with good power to increase or decrease aggregate demand. Because it can change private capital. Good fiscal policy in order to ensure it, it must prepare 2 fiscal budgets. The first one is for the normal functions of public administration. considered one of the most difficult decisions of the redistribution process.

It is also possible that some of Keynes's views affect private investments. But Wilson said that it was an incentive to increase aggregate demand. But other scientists say that it was aimed at creating semi-autonomous bodies.

Many scholars criticize Keynes' contribution to economic policy by emphasizing that fiscal policy and monetary policy can effectively affect aggregate demand. But Keynes spent much of his life trying to develop it by emphasizing monetary policy that would help create and maintain employment. According to Keynes, normal rates have nothing to do with natural rates or other concepts of this kind. Normality is a subjective concept and depends on the individual's experience. The diversity of views on what is normal is an important element in Keynes's liquidity preference theory of interest rates. And in some of his theories, he argued that interest rates should be lower than they actually are because people are affected by it, and that governments should always keep interest rates low. . Under these circumstances, Keynes noted: "If we know what rate of interest is required to make the flow of new projects profitable at the right rate, we have the power to make that rate prevail in the market."

Besides Keynesian monetary policy, he says something simple. Because after saying that the patient should intervene and manage, some of them describe his opinion as unusual. Because at that time, he ensures that the monetary policy should be provided with openness. That is, he emphasizes that there should be no secrecy at all in monetary and credit policy. That is, he says that after the government is given the government, the people will be aware of how it manages it, precisely in the monetary policy.

Maintaining a high level of aggregate demand at one point clearly increased the risk of inflationary pressures, and Keynes, contrary to popular opinion, did not ignore this and offered little solution. He had seen the danger of inflation.

The purpose of this article is to emphasize the presence of interventionist bias in Keynesian macroeconomics. Here, he emphasized the uncertainty of private property found in capitalism and the possibility of state intervention in the economy due to this. And in this article, the impact of Keynesian theory on the market was organized from the war, and what activities were carried out and the demand. Indeed, this paper suggests that Keynes' view of the need for macroeconomic policy stems from 2 sets of assumptions. First, the concept of money economy or money production economy is distinguished by the possibility of effective failure of demand, because unproduced money can dominate labor using capital assets as a means of accumulating wealth. Second, governments can assess the nature of these failures and attack them effectively. Keynes wrote in 1926: "The greatest economic evils of our time are the fruits of risk, uncertainty, and ignorance. Because some people of circumstance or ability are able to take advantage of uncertainty and ignorance, and for the same reason that big business is often a lottery. large inequalities of wealth arise; and it is these factors that cause the unemployment of labor or the frustration of the reasonable expectations of business, and the disruption of efficiency and production."

References.

BLAUG, M. (1990) John Maynard Keynes: Life, Ideas and Legacy. London, Macmillan. BOYER, R. (1985) The Influence of Keynes on French Economic Policy: Past and Present. In

Wattel, H. (ed.) The Policy Consequences of John Maynard Keynes. Armonk, ME Sharpe.

BUCHANAN, J. (1987) Keynesian Follies. ln Reese, D. (ed.) The Legacy of Keynes. San Francisco, Harper and Row.

CARVALHO, F. (1992) Mr. Keynes and the Post Keynesians. Cheltenham, Edward Elgar.

CUKIERMAN, A. (1994) Central Bank Independence and Monetary Control. The Economic Journal, November.

CUNNINGHAM, S. & VILASUSO, J. (1994/5) Is Keynesian Demand Management Policy Still Viable?. Journal of Post Keynesian Economics, 17 (2).

DAVIDSON, P. (1978) "Why Money Matters: Lessons from a Half-Century of Monetary Theory" Journal of Post Keynesian Economics, l (1).

HALL, P. (ed.) (1989b) The Political Power of Economic Ideas. Princeton, Princeton University Press.

HALL, P. (1989a) 'Introduction'. In Hall, P. (ed.), op. cit.

HAYEK. F. von (1949) Individualism and Economic Order. London, Routledge and Kegan Paul.

HUTCHISON, T. (1977) Keynes v. the Keynesians?. London, Institute of Economic Affairs.

KEYNES, JM The Collected Writings of John Maynard Keynes, 30 volumes. London, MacMillan and Cambridge, Cambridge University Press. Volumes are identified as.

3.2 Reasons and consequences of joining the World Trade Organization and the Republic of Uzbekistan.

WTO, that is, World Trade Organization, and WTO (World Trade Organization) in English, this organization was established in January 1995. This is what was written in Markosh's declaration of April 15, 1994. "Its results will strengthen the world economy and expand trade and investment worldwide, leading to increased employment and incomes. It is also a platform for developing trade relations between countries through collective discussions, negotiations and presentations." This organization was created on the basis of the agreements and contracts of 1994, that is, it includes intellectual property, service, and product sales of that year. 164 countries have been members of this organization for 27 years, and the doors of these countries are open to each other. About 20 agreements and related normative legal framework have been created. 164 countries that are members of the World Trade Organization must obey and fulfill these documents and agreements. Countries wishing to join must adapt their country to this structure. New projects or deals to be created in the organization are determined by general voting among all member states. Contracts and agreements are concluded depending on the number of votes collected in the charter. But this is only in the charter, because there has been no change or innovation with such an event in the history of the organization. According to the law, decisions are made and issued once every 2 years at the Ministerial Conference. Chiefs of staff or general managers meet and discuss once a year in the organization's building in Geneva. Representatives and ambassadors of member countries take part in meetings held in the organization. Employees work under the General Council to solve problems, analyze political and financial affairs, more than 650 employees work in the organization. In addition, it includes a trade and development committee, a trade balance restriction committee, and a budget, finance, and administrative committee. In addition to the main council, we have a lower governing body similar to the senate, which includes 3 councils; Council for Trade in Goods, Council for Services and Council for Intellectual Property Rights. The director of the organization is currently Ngozi Okondjo-Iweala. There are 3 main languages of the organization: English, French and Spanish. Employees work under the General Council to solve problems, analyze political and financial affairs, more than 650 employees work in the organization. In addition, it includes a trade and development committee, a trade balance restriction committee, and a budget, finance, and administrative committee. In addition to the main council, we have a lower governing body similar to the senate, which includes 3 councils; Council for Trade in Goods, Council for Services and Council for Intellectual Property Rights. The director of the organization is currently Ngozi Okondjo-Iweala. There are 3 main languages of the organization: English, French and Spanish. Employees work under the General Council to solve problems, analyze political and financial affairs, more than 650 employees work in the organization. In addition, it includes a trade and development committee, a trade balance restriction committee, and a budget, finance, and administrative committee. In addition to the main council, we have a lower governing body similar to the senate, which includes 3 councils; Council for Trade in Goods, Council for Services and Council for Intellectual Property Rights. The director of the organization is currently Ngozi Okondjo-Iweala. There are 3 main languages of the organization: English, French and Spanish. more than 650 employees work in the organization. In addition, it includes a trade and development committee, a trade balance restriction committee, and a budget, finance, and administrative committee. In addition to the main council, we have a lower governing body similar to the senate, which includes 3 councils; Council for Trade in Goods, Council for Services and Council for Intellectual Property Rights. The director of the organization is currently Ngozi Okondjo-Iweala. There are 3 main languages of the organization: English, French and Spanish. more than 650 employees work in the organization. In addition, it includes a trade and development committee, a trade balance restriction committee, and a budget, finance, and administrative committee. In addition to the main council, we have a lower governing body similar to the senate, which includes 3 councils; Council for Trade in Goods, Council for Services and Council for Intellectual Property Rights. The director of the organization is currently Ngozi Okondjo-Iweala. There are 3 main languages of the organization: English, French and Spanish. In addition to the main council, we have a lower governing body similar to the senate, which includes 3 councils; Council for Trade in Goods, Council for Services and Council for Intellectual Property Rights. The director of the organization is currently Ngozi Okondjo-Iweala. There are 3 main languages of the organization: English, French and Spanish. In addition to the main council, we have a lower governing body similar to the senate, which includes 3 councils; Council for Trade in Goods, Council for Services and Council for Intellectual Property Rights. The director of the organization is currently Ngozi Okondjo-Iweala. There are 3 main languages of the organization: English, French and Spanish.

Today, there are 5 main principles of the WTO:

1) Non-discrimination. That is, not treating a country based on its nationality, religion or military power means that they should have the same rights and obligations as all member states to open free trade routes. At the same time, imported goods should be placed alongside products produced by domestic producers and should not be separated in the markets.

2) Mutual friendship. It includes establishing access to foreign markets and free trade in land for member states, and improving and developing relations among member states, i.e. 164 countries.

3) Obligations imposed and enforceable. In this case, it is understood that it is necessary to fulfill the burdens imposed on joining the organization, i.e. ensuring the import goods policy,

customs duties and other taxes. In addition, trading partners cannot update or change the agreements themselves. They themselves must innovate according to the agreement between the 2 partners.

4) Transparency. The member states of the organization must always provide information about the provisions of their laws or deliver the amended laws to the general council and maintain and develop tax institutions in their state and receive information from other states, i.e. trade and taxes. should respond to inquiries received on time, speed and accuracy.

5) Security. In some cases, member states may restrict trade. According to the WTO agreement, member states are obliged to protect and develop not only the environment, but also the health of people, animals and plants.

It takes different countries to join this organization. For example, 8 - 10 or 10-15 or 15-20 years (the record was set by the Kyrgyz Republic in 1998 in 2 years and 10 months. Russia became a member of the WTO in 20 years) .

The benefits of joining the WTO are purely economic. That is, to increase and maximize the exchange of goods between countries without any restrictions, and to implement new technologies, develop them, introduce them to large and small businesses, and maximize profit from them.

It helps to improve the standard of living of the population and significantly increases people's ability to buy and consume high-quality and many different types of products at a lower price.

It increases the volume of exports, which helps to raise the Gross Domestic Product, and helps to reduce the price of national products in exported goods. Develops national production, helps to increase revenue to the budget. Trade liberalization helps to increase the income of the country and individual people.

It has a positive effect on employment, i.e. it improves it. The openness of many countries helps people to work in other countries and increase their income.

However, not all of these opportunities and these things are available in every country. If there is no production, natural resources, intellectual knowledge and economic growth in a particular country, there will be no change. For example, even though the Kyrgyz Republic has been a member of the World Trade Organization for 24 years, there is still no sign of a prosperous life.

Kyrgyz ambassador Mukhtar Jumaliev also modestly evaluated the success of the republic at the event in Washington.

"I cannot say that the membership has harmed Kyrgyzstan. Since 1998, foreign trade has increased sixfold. However, it must be admitted that 60% of the trade volume is accounted for by Russia, Kazakhstan and Uzbekistan. we trade with countries on the basis of bilateral agreements. Investments have increased, but we have not seen that this is due to membership. Our presence in the World Trade Organization has greatly developed the services sector. Including telecommunications, transport, energy supply, etc. ", - says the Kyrgyz ambassador.

According to Mukhtar Jumaliev, the biggest benefit was in resolving trade disputes. It is easier and faster for small countries to solve problems within the framework of the organization than through bilateral agreements, he said in his speech.

According to many scientists and economists, Kyrgyzstan will develop when. The benefit of the WTO will be felt only if its closest neighbors and partners join the World Trade Organization. Currently, Russia and Kazakhstan have joined the World Trade Organization, but Uzbekistan, which is the largest partner, has not. Regional trade will increase and investors will be able to invest without fear.

Kyrgyzstan quickly dismayed its neighbors by joining the organization in 1998, flooding the Kyrgyz market with low-quality goods and forcing Uzbekistan and Kazakhstan to raise tariffs. Kyrgyzstan's trade with its 2 main partners has been limited. This information is included in the minuses of the WTO, that is, small countries cannot use all the opportunities like giant countries.

Accession to the WTO will greatly affect the domestic system of the countries. Small businesses and established businesses are at a very high risk of bankruptcy. After the removal of protectionism, large companies in the country can also go into huge debt, because in many countries the firms are still not equipped with modern technologies and modern knowledge.

Why Uzbekistan has not become a member of the WTO. It's been a long time since 1994. After receiving the application for joining the WTO, each country is studied separately and a decision is made accordingly. The process takes an average of 5 years, and during this period the organization examines the country's trade balances, fiscal policy, and the right decision is made. If tax policies do not change during this year, political issues affect or conditions are not met, this period will be extended. After Uzbekistan's application in 1994, the government began to change its policy, but after 1995, the decrease of Uzbekistan's exports and prices in world trade caused the country to further strengthen protectionism. And the government begins to reduce imports with currency controls. The recession in Asian countries in 1998 will strengthen protectionism again. In 2003, currency restrictions will be removed and the transition to a free trade system will begin. These reforms helped the country's economy grow quickly. But the collapse of the world economy in 2008, unfortunately, had a strong impact on Uzbekistan, and the state again established currency control, and the market again switched to protectionism. There was a huge difference between the official course and the unofficial course, it was equally different, and for this reason, Uzbekistan could not join the WTO, and another reason for this is the events of Andijan in 2005, because after that event, Uzbekistan's international and foreign financial relations with institutions have deteriorated. In 2003, currency restrictions will be removed and the transition to a free trade system will begin. These reforms helped the country's economy grow quickly. But the collapse of the world economy in 2008, unfortunately, had a strong impact on Uzbekistan, and the state again established currency control, and the market again switched to protectionism. There was a huge difference between the official course and the unofficial course, it was equally different, and for this reason, Uzbekistan could not join the WTO, and another reason for this is the events of Andijan in 2005, because after that event, Uzbekistan's international and foreign financial relations with institutions have deteriorated. In 2003, currency restrictions will be removed and the transition to a free trade system will begin. These reforms helped the country's economy grow quickly. But the collapse of the world economy in 2008, unfortunately, had a strong impact on Uzbekistan, and the state again established currency control, and the market again switched to protectionism. There was a huge difference between the official course and the unofficial course, it was equally different, and for this reason, Uzbekistan could not join the WTO, and another reason for this is the events of Andijan in 2005, because after that event, Uzbekistan's international and foreign financial relations with institutions have deteriorated. But the collapse of the world economy in 2008, unfortunately, had a strong impact on Uzbekistan, and the state again established currency control, and the market again switched to protectionism. There was a huge difference between the official course and the unofficial course, it was equally different, and for this reason, Uzbekistan could not join the WTO, and another reason for this is the events of Andijan in 2005, because after that event, Uzbekistan's international and foreign financial relations with institutions have deteriorated. But the collapse of the world economy in 2008, unfortunately, had a strong impact on Uzbekistan, and the state again established currency control, and the market again switched to protectionism. There was a huge difference between the official course and the unofficial course, it was equally different, and for this reason, Uzbekistan could not join the WTO, and another reason for this is the events of Andijan in 2005, because after that event, Uzbekistan's international and foreign financial relations with institutions have deteriorated.

After the change of president in 2017, the foreign exchange market works on supply and demand, transition to a market economy, and from 2019, the government took control and strengthened the work of the task force working to join the WTO. According to resolution 1040 of 2018, a working group council on the inclusion of the country in the WTO has been formed, and the measures will be taken as soon as possible.

Summary

Why Uzbekistan still cannot join the World Trade Organization. To join the WTO, it is necessary to develop small businesses first and develop large companies. We know that most of the economy of Uzbekistan is specialized in agriculture and most of the people make a living from it, so unemployment does not affect the economy very much. Almost half of Uzbekistan's 6 million unemployed people benefit from agriculture, and if it joins the WTO, this income may decrease and increase unemployment. But this is very useful for countries with a raw material base, because nowadays raw materials solve a lot of things. For example, the closure of the hom-Asian base in Russia is a loss for the countries of the European Union.

Used resources

1. https://xs.uz/uz/post/zhahon-savdo-tashkiloti-azolik-uzbekistanga-nima-beradi.

2. https://www.jst.com/

3. One recent empirical reference is Frankel (1997). Theoretical discussions can be found in Deardorff (1998) and Anderson and van Wincoop (2002).

4. Available at http://www.wto.org/english/tratop_e/region_e/region_e.htm

5.16 Available at http://www.wto.org/english/thewto_e/gattmem_e.htm

6. Indeed, the first stage shows that countries inside the GATT/WTO have significantly higher output.

7. Economist, December 2, 1999

3.3 The Role of Digital Finance and Technological Innovation in the Growth of the Green Economy

Introduction

The global community is facing an urgent need to transition towards a green economy to address the environmental challenges and ensure sustainable development. The integration of digital finance and technological innovation has emerged as a promising approach to achieve this goal. Digital finance can provide new financing channels for green projects, while technological innovation can enhance the efficiency and effectiveness of green production and consumption.

The trend towards digital finance and technological innovation in the development of green economy is gaining momentum. Governments, international organizations, and private sector entities are increasingly investing in green technologies and digital finance solutions. The use of blockchain technology, artificial intelligence, and the internet of things (IoT) is enhancing the transparency, accountability, and traceability of green investments.

Moreover, digital finance is enabling the mobilization of capital for green projects from a wider range of investors, including retail investors. This is promoting inclusiveness and democratization of green finance. Technological innovations are also enhancing the efficiency and effectiveness of green production and consumption, reducing waste, improving resource utilization, and promoting circular economy principles.

However, the integration of digital finance and technological innovation in the development of green economy also presents challenges. These include issues related to data privacy, cybersecurity, and responsible use of technology. There is a need for robust regulatory frameworks to ensure the responsible use of technology and prevent any negative impacts on society or the environment.

Computer Trends

The three Vs of big data are variety, volume, and velocity. The operation and service patterns of established industries have changed as a result of the integration and innovation of big data and other sectors, and new platforms, new models, and new business forms have emerged, such as Internet banking and automobile sharing. The sharing and openness of large data has also accelerated mass innovation and entrepreneurship. Technological advancement and economic advancement that is driven by technology accelerate the digital economy. Traditional industries may increase their productivity and innovation capacity and accomplish their digital transformation with the advancement of big data technology and the integration of various social economy sectors.

New Blockchain Development Trend

The core of blockchain is a distributed accounting, synchronous updating ledger system that works in a decentralized, trustless manner to maintain a trustworthy database. Blockchain is essentially an unchangeable distributed ledger that serves as the foundational technology for Bitcoin. It also represents a whole new distributed infrastructure and computer paradigm. Its fundamental concepts include the use of distributed networks to achieve decentralized information processing, consensus mechanisms to build trust between nodes, asymmetric encryption, and redundant distributed storage to achieve information security, and blockchain data structures to achieve data information traceability.

The following are the blockchain's current development trends in the age of the digital economy: The virtual blockchain will first be converted into a physical blockchain. Currency speculation will slow down, and blockchain's capabilities for establishing trust will be taken seriously and implemented in the real world to boost the effectiveness of the real economy. And last, cross-fusion. The integration of emerging digital technologies like big data, the Internet of Things, and artificial intelligence will be accelerated by blockchain. Big data, the Internet of Things, artificial intelligence, and other next-generation information technologies are needed to enable the development of blockchain technology and applications as well as to broaden the application field. in the meantime, the advancement of blockchain technology and applications is crucial for the growth of the next generation of the information technology sector. Third, blockchain development driven by standards will be more uniform. The blockchain technology market has experienced rapid growth, but due to differences in the market, between users, a lack of uniform standards, duplication, and resource waste, China's Ministry of Industry marked the blockchain technology standardization stage in essence in February 2018.

Despite the fact that blockchain technology is still in its early stages of development and has only a small number of applications currently, there are still several issues. The digital economy management platform based on blockchain is anticipated to become a public data sharing management infrastructure, and blockchain technology will gradually become the mainstream of the application. As it spreads from the financial sector to the non-financial sector penetration, it will gradually become a new demand that subverts the traditional business model.

VR's Newest Developmental Trend

Virtual reality (VR) is based on data collection, computer three-dimensional graphics, multimedia, interpersonal interaction, network transmission, three-dimensional display, and other technologies that have been combined to create a new technology. Big data may offer detailed support for an immersive virtual environment as the digital economy develops, and virtual reality offers extensive visualization options for big data. People's capacity to process and evaluate interactive large data is improved in this way.

The development of virtual reality technology has brought forth new industrial shifts and economic prospects in the age of the digital economy. The use and advancement of virtual reality in industrial design, virtual commerce, psychological therapy and rehabilitation, military simulation, and other sectors has been fueled by the digital economy. To solve the issues that conventional 2D and 3D visualization systems are unable to process due to complex datasets, MIT Multimedia Experiment Center, Virtualitics, and other research institutions apply big data technology to VR scene construction, maximizing the inherent benefits of VR (immersion). Based on NASDAQ data, the virtual realm of the rollercoaster gives riders a first-person perspective of NASDAQ's ascent and decline over the last 21 years. Master of Pie showed how VR can be used in big data analytics, where users can instantly examine and change data since it is presented in a more realistic and engaging way. According to Forbes, big data analysts utilizing the technology can view four times as much data as they could on a standard computer screen "at a glance."

A New Sharing Economy Development Trend

The sharing economy, a new business model based on big data, cloud computing, and third-party payment, has emerged quickly as a result of the rapid expansion of mobile internet. The goal of the sharing economy is to eliminate conventional merchants, and digitization is what propels this elimination process forward. In order to increase service availability, lower transaction costs, and give customers access to the features of productive services, digital technology makes it participate in the transaction process through point-to-point connections. For instance, bike-sharing and car-sharing are expanding quickly in terms of shared transportation. According to Didi Chuxing's operational data for 2017, there were more than 20 billion route planning requests completed daily, totaling more than 4500 TB. Data analysis may help in environmentally friendly travel, smart travel, and better urban planning. According to research, Airbnb can house an average of 400,000 guests every night and has more than 120 million listings in more than 190 countries. The rise of the digital economy is accelerated by the sharing economy's rapid development. Accurate matching is accomplished by analysis and prediction based on the vast amounts of data provided by the sharing economy, accelerating the growth of the sharing economy. A decision-making framework for urban development may be established based on the vast amounts of data created by the sharing economy, which can also be used to assess the current situation and evolving trends in urban employment, transportation, education, health care, and other livelihoods. In the future, the sharing economy will progressively extend to a wide range of industries, particularly important ones like education and health care. It will also carry out derivative activities, encourage more cross-border collaboration and innovation, and further expand its dimensions and service chain. The sharing economy will likewise progressively expand to encompass the entire process, from consumption and production to distribution and circulation.

The Internet of things is rapidly developing, enabling a range of sensors and terminals to connect to the network and connect collectively. The quantity and makeup of Internet-connected devices have both risen dramatically concurrently, from PC to mobile phone to tablet to the Internet of Things era. The pressing requirement to assess unstructured data results from this evolution. According to estimates, there will be 50 billion connected sensing devices in 2020, creating 2.5 million terabytes of data daily, or 2.38 times as much as the current Internet. The Internet of Things is being used more quickly in areas including clinical observation frameworks, smart home machine control, and operations and production network following because of the combination of the Internet of Things with the modern economy. In the age of the digital economy, the Internet of Things has generally advanced in the following ways: First, high precision sensor development is being developed to increase information transmission and collection in general. The popularity of wearable technology increases the mobility of the Internet of Things, while high-precision sensor development improves observational awareness and accuracy. Second, it can work in tandem with smart devices to enhance the Internet of things' cognitive capabilities. In order to grasp the continuous monitoring administration of the client's body and prevent the occurrence of linked illnesses, the monitoring data of smart watches/wristbands in wearable gadgets may be supplied to the medical clinic gradually. Third, the biological system of the Internet of Things has evolved into the main form of utilization landing. The IoT biological system has also been arranged in a progressive manner by IT behemoths. Apple, for instance, has designed a multi-stage IoT ecosystem that includes smart home HomeKit, wearable device HealthKit, and automobile IoT CarPlay. Project IoT was offered by Google, which also provided the basic IoT working framework known as Brillo. Huawei has provided Lite OS, a compact Internet of Things operating system, and NB-IoT, a complete solution for setting up an Ocean Connect environment.

New Trends in AI Development

The accumulation of computerized resources, the increase in processing speed, and the improvement of organizational offices have transformed the flood of vast information from a science fiction to a reality, and man-made brainpower is now entering a new phase of cross-line combination with significant application and influencing turn of events. The Federal Bureau of Investigation (FBI) established the FACE dataset (NGI), which contains the fingerprints, irises, faces, and other biometric data of 117 million adult Americans. Face recognition technology may be used to identify the target through photos. Man-made reasoning innovation may be used in the clinical area to manage the enormous amounts of data and information obtained, identify the crucial cases and key premise, and improve the precision of conclusion and navigation. Then, deep learning and artificial intelligence will be increasingly vital to both computer economy and human consciousness innovation. Accelerate the use of program-driven, clinical, and common sense computer thinking in money, fostering a new wave of contemporary change.

Cross-disciplinary innovation and integration in the age of the digital economy

Its core components are data resources, the essential technology of data mining, and resource utilization. Its essence is large data, cloud computing, Internet of things, artificial intelligence, and blockchain: five new digital technologies that are driving the digital transformation. The digital economy is the economic sector that is currently growing the most quickly and widely.

Big data technology helps the sharing economy industry innovate and grow, but it also has many drawbacks, including poor regulation, information security, and privacy issues. Relying solely on big data sharing technology has prevented the development of new economic models, while blockchain technology has encryption sharing, which does not compromise the benefits. It offers new technological assistance for the transfer and exchange of data, and it can work in conjunction with big data technologies. In the age of big data, blockchain technology offers three features: First, the value and application space of blockchain data are enhanced by big data mass storage and distributed computing technologies.

Blockchain offers a solid assurance for the open exchange of big data under the presumption of privacy protection, liberating additional large data, thanks to its dependability, security, and immutability. Second, the traceability aspects of blockchain may significantly enhance the quality of data. As a result, the quality of the data has a high confidence endorsement. Blockchain can record every stage of data processing in full, including data gathering, transaction, circulation, and computational analysis. Third, standardizing data use and adjusting authorization scope are both possible with blockchain. Desensitization-induced data trading and circulation can stop information islands from forming and encourage the gradual development of globalized data trading scenarios. The effective integration of the digital economy with blockchain technology and the Internet of Things will also usher in a new round of economic revolution. the traceability aspects of blockchain may significantly enhance the quality of data. As a result, the quality of the data has a high confidence endorsement. Blockchain can record every stage of data processing in full, including data gathering, transaction, circulation, and computational analysis. Third, standardizing data use and adjusting authorization scope are both possible with blockchain. Desensitization-induced data trading and circulation can stop information islands from forming and encourage the gradual development of globalized data trading scenarios. The effective integration of the digital economy with blockchain technology and the Internet of Things will also usher in a new round of economic revolution. the traceability aspects of blockchain may significantly enhance the quality of data. As a result, the quality of the data has a high confidence endorsement. Blockchain can record every stage of data processing in full, including data gathering, transaction, circulation, and computational analysis. Third, standardizing data use and adjusting authorization scope are both possible with blockchain. Desensitization-induced data trading and circulation can stop information islands from forming and encourage the gradual development of globalized data trading scenarios. The effective integration of the digital economy with blockchain technology and the Internet of Things will also usher in a new round of economic revolution. the quality of the data has a high confidence endorsement. Blockchain can record every stage of data processing in full, including data gathering, transaction, circulation, and computational analysis. Third, standardizing data use and adjusting authorization scope are both possible with blockchain. Desensitization-induced data trading and circulation can stop information islands from forming and encourage the gradual development of globalized data trading scenarios. The effective integration of the digital economy with blockchain technology and the Internet of Things will also usher in a new round of economic revolution. the quality of the data has a high confidence endorsement. Blockchain can record every stage of data processing in full, including data gathering, transaction, circulation, and computational analysis. Third, standardizing data use and adjusting authorization scope are both possible with blockchain. Desensitization-induced data trading and circulation can stop information islands from forming and encourage the gradual development of globalized data trading scenarios. The effective integration of the digital economy with blockchain technology and the Internet of Things will also usher in a new round of economic revolution. standardizing data use and adjusting authorization scope are both possible with blockchain. Desensitization-induced data trading and circulation can stop information islands from forming and encourage the gradual development of globalized data trading scenarios. The effective integration of the digital economy with blockchain technology and the Internet of Things will also usher in a new round of economic revolution. standardizing data use and adjusting authorization scope are both possible with blockchain. Desensitization-induced data trading and circulation can stop information islands from forming and encourage the gradual development of globalized data trading scenarios. The effective integration of the digital economy with blockchain technology and the Internet of Things will also usher in a new round of economic revolution.

The Creative Development of the Digital Economy is Supported by the Integration of New Digital Technologies

Its core components are data resources, the essential technology of data mining, and resource utilization. Its essence is large data, cloud computing, network, artificial intelligence, and blockchain—five new technologies that are accelerating the digital transformation of the economy. The digital economy is the one that is currently growing the fastest. Because of the fundamental changes that new digital technologies have brought about in human thought, production, and daily life, economic digitalization has become a key driver of creative economic growth.

Trends in Application Innovation in the Digital Economy

"Tmall International," with over 40 million service users, controls half of China's online retail business. Tmall International relies on Alibaba's powerful data ecosystem in this retail ecosystem based on the Internet and big data to assist a large number of foreign merchants in breaking through the brand online and offline system and establishing a global supply chain. Brand operators, such as Swisse, an Australian natural health brand, exchange data with Alibaba in order to forecast customer purchasing habits and possible demand. Figure 1 depicts the new retail applications that have emerged in the digital economy. The new retail sector has grown to be a trillion-dollar business, with each major taking the lead. "Hema Xiansheng" is an example of a typical representation. It employs digital technology and comprehensive performance links in the supply chain, sales, and logistics to achieve full digital, intelligent, optimized workflow, reduce ineffective work, and shop for their goods, shelves, picking, packing, distribution, and other tasks, which can be identified by intelligent devices; the error rate is extremely low, and the entire system is divided into foreground and background. Users submit purchases within 10 minutes of sorting and packaging, and delivery within 3 kilometers takes 20 minutes. and the entire system is divided into foreground and background. Users submit purchases within 10 minutes of sorting and packaging, and delivery within 3 kilometers takes 20 minutes. and the entire system is divided into foreground and background. Users submit purchases within 10 minutes of sorting and packaging, and delivery within 3 kilometers takes 20 minutes.

Digital New Technology Drives Manufacturing and Production to Realize Intelligent Production. The Internet of Things (IoT) combines artificial intelligence, cloud computing, and big data analytics to analyze data collected by a large number of connected sensors that can monitor complex physical and mechanical performance in real time to optimize production and perform proactive maintenance, improving efficiency, and generating information that can be used to develop new processes. The obtained data may also be utilized to study other crucial areas outside of production, such as lowering energy use and investing in network resources. In product production planning and process control, the factory uses smart devices and sensors to collect large amounts of data from the manufacturing process, dig into these data and applications, and optimize processing methods, processing sequence, and system technology indexes such as cutting parameters, real-time monitoring of the manufacturing process, troubleshooting, and feedback adjustment. Digital New Technology Drives Operation Optimization and Lean Management. Through the Internet of things, the manufacturing process, equipment operating conditions, process parameters, and other information can be gathered in real time, and product quality and faults can be identified and quantified. Machine learning technology is employed offline to mine the association between product problems and historical data from the Internet of Things and develop control rules. It can regulate the manufacturing process in the online state by using improved learning technologies and real-time feedback to eliminate product flaws. At the same time, it may include expert knowledge to constantly enhance learning outcomes. In the maintenance service link, sensors are used to monitor the status of the equipment, and machine learning is used to create an analytical model of the equipment failure. Before the failure occurs, the potentially failing workpiece is changed to ensure the equipment's ongoing trouble-free functioning. To increase inventory efficiency, firms may utilize geographic big data analysis technology to integrate and optimize supply chain distribution networks, optimize purchase time, purchase amount, warehouse allocation, and so on. Artificial intelligence may also be employed in digital field equipment life cycle health management, machine vision-based field safety, field environmental management, and other areas of field management optimization.

New Smart City Application Trend

The wisdom of city development is inextricably linked to the construction of urban informatization infrastructure; infrastructure to collect and record large data resources for professional analysis and management decision support is required; and, to some extent, blocking the use of chain technology can solve urban problems such as data storage and safety. McKinsey predicted in a research report based on Western industry data that the use of big data would save governments in European developed countries more than 100 billion euros in operating costs and reduce medical insurance costs in the United States by 8%, saving more than $300 billion annually.

Digital New Technology Will Realize the Scientific Development of the Urban Economic Structure, Spatial Structure, and Social Structure.

Big data, in particular, as an important strategic asset in urban planning, is conducive to the cultivation of a new concept of urban planning combining "top-down" and "bottom-up" approaches, and can promote the realization of a new trend of integrating GIS-based urban planning systems into urban planning. Innovative data collecting and processing technologies, on-site research methodologies, new programming methods, public engagement in planning, and new urban planning methods will ultimately propel smart city planning to new heights and establish a progressive smart city planning system.

Accurate Management of Urban Social Order, Ecological Environment, and Infrastructure Can Be Achieved Using Digital New Technology

Artificial intelligence's intelligent observation and recognition technology may be used to collect and coordinate real-time data on urban traffic, logistics, energy, the environment, and other topics. The digital intelligent administration of the city will eventually actualize the intelligent allocation of public resources, thanks to the data-driven construction of urban decision-making mechanisms. It can automatically digest the unstructured large surveillance video data created by the security business that cannot be calculated statistically using artificial intelligence technologies. Artificial intelligence has now infiltrated every sector and functions to varying degrees. It can do intelligent analyzes and efficiently use urban information by collecting data in many sectors, improving the efficiency of urban management, saving resources,

New Digital Technology Aids in the Prevention and Management of Chronic Disease

A national public health monitoring platform will be constructed using the Internet of Things. Through a nationwide electronic medical record database, health departments may improve continuous medical observation, identify potential illness risks in real time, provide early warning, and avoid chronic diseases and epidemics. Furthermore, patients' personal data, electronic medical records, and ethnic databases in China may be utilized to promptly detect ailments and identify causes, allowing for the development of customized rehabilitation therapy plans tailored to Chinese people. "Shuangquan (comprehensive screening and whole-process management)

Plan" and Google's "Global Influenza Map" are key expressions of big data in the administration of mass prevention and treatment of chronic diseases, as well as the forecast of high occurrence regions. Finally, by merging the Internet of Things with blockchain, all types of medical equipment and services may be linked to track residents' and patients' exercise and health data, as well as get fitness, medical, physical, and exercise monitoring data. Blockchain anonymity protects patients' privacy. It may also pass over the information channel between hospitals, financial insurance, pharmaceutical manufacturers, and other important departments at the same time. Blockchain anonymity protects patients' privacy. It may also pass over the information channel between hospitals, financial insurance, pharmaceutical manufacturers, and other important departments at the same time. Blockchain anonymity protects patients' privacy. It may also pass over the information channel between hospitals, financial insurance, pharmaceutical manufacturers, and other important departments at the same time.

New Digital Technologies to Aid Clinical Decision Making.

To achieve precision medicine, artificial intelligence technology is used to analyze diverse, multi-source, fragmented, and unstructured medical data and to support clinical decision-making through a variety of means such as etiology identification, clinical data comparison, clinical decision support, and remote patient data analysis. In terms of clinical data comparison, matching the medication status of patients of the same kind yields the optimal treatment method. Deep learning and other algorithms are used on medical datasets in clinical decision support to provide intelligent diagnosis and therapy. New Digital Technology Aids Medical Research and Develop

The pharmaceutical research and development business may be freed from the conundrum of high investment, high risk, and long cycle thanks to the integration of big data into every stage of medical research and development. Big data can also play a crucial role in every step of research and development. The impact of big data on the whole medication R&D process may be seen in three stages through data summary and analysis: During the drug project approval stage, we used big data to identify drugs that were urgently needed in the market, quickly analyzed pre-clinical trials of drugs, identified effective target drugs, and analyzed technology to process drug data (for example, there are nearly 30 diabetes drugs on the market worldwide, with each drug having approximately 20,000 pages of literature). Chemical structure big data may be utilized in the drug development stage to quickly generate chemical structures or perform targeted structural transformations, compare pharmaceutical processes, and optimize pharmaceutical processes. Big data from clinical trials may be used to create pharmacodynamic models, evaluate efficacy, predict bad responses, and speed up clinical trials throughout the clinical trial stage.

Personalized Education Application: A New Trend

The new digital technology has the scientific power to encourage educational innovation and progress. Educational big data is a collection of all the data created during the whole process of educational activities and gathered in accordance with educational demands for educational progress, and it has enormous potential value. New digital technologies such as blockchain and artificial intelligence, driven by big data in education, are becoming a subversive force to stimulate innovation and transform the education system. In comparison to traditional education, the implementation of personalized education applications is dependent on the use of modern digital technologies in the following areas.

New digital technologies assist learners in discovering and developing their potential, as well as improving their academic performance.

Educational Artificial Intelligence (EAI) is a new area that combines artificial intelligence with learning research. A huge number of educational AI systems are now being used in classrooms. To promote customized learning, these systems incorporate educational AI and educational data mining (EDM) technology (such as machine learning algorithms) to track students' behavioral data and forecast their learning achievement. "Teaching, learning, and evaluation" may be naturally blended using artificial intelligence. Schools and other institutions can use NLPs and other artificial intelligence technologies to automatically mark learning materials in order to evaluate students' knowledge points, provide real-time feedback and correct evaluation, and encourage learning through collaborative supervision and self-supervision.

Teachers can use new digital technology to determine the most effective teaching method and optimize the teaching process.

Big data matching algorithms help in the realization of learning recommendations, the analysis of learning data and course data, and the realization of adaptive learning. For example, the Knewton corporation in the United States has leveraged big data to provide digital course materials, resulting in dynamic and ongoing customization to each student's specific needs. Big data behavior analysis means are continuously boosting conventional education from statistical analysis for groups to behavior analysis for individuals as Internet technology continues to permeate the education business. After collecting large amounts of data, intelligent approaches such as association analysis and recommendation algorithms may be used to modify individualized instructional materials and procedures, automatically find rules, and anticipate them. For example, "Xuetang Online" can investigate the value of

MOOCs and modify courses accordingly. On the other hand, based on online and offline data analysis, it can help pupils solve difficulties more quickly. Real-time feedback on learning data is useful for exploring students' interests and traits, enabling the sharing of online and offline data, supervised learning, judging students' knowledge mastery, and promptly modifying teaching ideas and techniques.

The new digital technology contributes to the realization of the paradigm of two-way education delivery. Teaching content may be structured using virtual reality technology according to their own thoughts and knowledge structure, and this organizing information is not a basic linear structure. Virtual reality technology combines these complex pieces of knowledge into a network, giving pupils a realistic knowledge structure. It includes not only the subject's fundamental material, but also the logical link between the subject's contents. It focuses on both the process of knowledge generation and the structure of knowledge. The unity and flexibility of the educational content may be precisely blended by coordinating our vision, hearing, and touch. Virtual reality may be restored to actual situations for many abstract concepts and objects,

A New Trend in Regional Tourism Application

With the advent of mass tourism, new digital technology is becoming increasingly crucial in the tourist business. The growth of regional tourism must rely on new digital technology to make judgments rather than on perceptual experience.

LBS, search engine, online travel agency (OTA), and other tourist data can help in market segmentation and positioning in the tourism business. The tourist climate index, in particular, may be used to forecast future tourism market growth. The tourism market is categorized based on the preferences of travelers. The dispersion of major tourist source markets may be judged using tourist source analysis. We can investigate the depression of regional tourism markets by analyzing prospective markets, and we can increase the tourism market conversion rate by analyzing visitor loss.

We can integrate various tourism-related businesses and professional resources, acquire big data, accurately analyze, integrate, and share the obtained data, and provide strong support for tourism managers to make decisions and meet the personalized needs of tourists using the Internet of Things technology and cloud computing platform. Building user portraits, personalized tourism strategy recommendation, and innovation of traditional tourism department organizational forms, such as personalized recommendation matching destinations, tourist attractions, and routes, personalized recommendation of hotels and locations, personalized recommendation of direct flight or transfer, and personalized recommendation of popular food and shopping sites, can all be accomplished. TripAdvisor has performed admirably in this regard.

The number of visitors prediction and safety warning may be determined using weather, hotel, traffic, and other data. Deeply analyze the scenic spot's daily, weekly, seasonal, and holiday traffic characteristics, as well as the impact of weather, traffic, and historical traffic data on the scenic spot, and then control the distribution of tourists in the scenic spot based on real time on the scenic spot forecast and legal holiday traffic, in order to effectively prevent tourists from crowding and stampeding in the scenic spot.

Conclusion

In conclusion, the integration of digital finance and technological innovation is a promising approach to promote the development of green economy. The application of digital finance can provide new financing channels for green projects, while technological innovation can enhance the efficiency and effectiveness of green production and consumption. However, there are still challenges that need to be addressed, such as the need for regulatory frameworks and the potential risk of technology being misused. Therefore, it is important to continue exploring and promoting the development of digital finance and technological innovation in the green economy, with a focus on sustainability, inclusivity, and responsible use of technology.

References

1 Gray, C. (2000). "Formality, Intentionality, and Planning: Features of Successful Entrepreneurial SMEs in the Future?" paper presented at the ICSB World Conference 2000, Brisbane, Australia, June.

2 Maki, K., and T. Pukkinen (2000). "Barriers to Growth and Employment in Finnish Small Enterprises," paper presented at the ICSB World Conference 2000, Brisbane, Australia, June.

3 Mitra, J., and H. Matlay (2000). "Toward the New Millennium: The Growth Potential of Innovative SMEs," paper presented at the ICSB World Conference, Brisbane, Australia, June.

4 Small Business Administration (2000). History of the US Small Business Administration, http://www.sba.gov (Accessed 25 May 2001)

5 Storey, D. (1994). Understanding Small Business. London: Routledge.

6 Stanworth, J., and J. Curran (1976). "Growth and the Smaller Firm—An Alternative View," Journal of Management Studies 13(May), 95–110

F. Guo, ST Kong, and J. Wang, "General patterns and regional disparity of internet finance development in China: evidence from the Peking University internet finance development index," China Economic Journal, vol. 9, 2016.

R. Nanda and T. Nicholas, "Did bank distress stifle innovation during the great depression?" Journal of Financial Economics, vol. 114, no. 2, pp. 273–292, 2014.

J. Schor and C. Fitzmaurice, "Collaborating and connecting: the emergence of the sharing economy," Handbook on Research on Sustainable Consumption, Edward Elgar Publishing, Cheltenham, UK, p. 410, 2015.

JA Schumpter, Capitalism, Socialism and Democracy, New York: Harper: Harper & Brothers, NewYork, NY, USA, 1942.

JA Schumpter, Capitalism, Socialism and Democracy, New York: Harper: Harper & Brothers, NewYork, NY, USA, 1942.

F. Guo, ST Kong, and J. Wang, "General patterns and regional disparity of internet finance development in China: evidence from the Peking University internet finance development index," China Economic Journal, vol. 9, 2016.

Written on the topic of the development of the economy in Uzbekistan, this book consists of an introduction, a main chapter and a conclusion, and is covered in the form of economic accounts and specific facts.

www.ingramcontent.com/pod-product-compliance
Lightning Source LLC
LaVergne TN
LVHW020450070526
838199LV00063B/4906